Fish On

The Further Chronicles
of Bouncer Smith

By

Captain Bouncer Smith
As Told to
Patrick Mansell

Fish On

The Further Chronicles of Bouncer Smith

By

Captain Bouncer Smith
As Told to Patrick Mansell

©2019 By Randolph "Bouncer" Smith
and Patrick Mansell

ISBN 978-0-9898738-7-1

Dedication

This book is dedicated to all the friends, relatives, clients, and followers who have supported me in my life and career as a fisherman, captain, and guide. Your loving support and guidance has made my Lifetime of Fishing unique, fulfilling, and epic. You have given me more than any one man deserves, and I am eternally grateful that I have been fortunate enough to share my adventures with you.

Table of Contents

Introduction

When the original Bouncer Smith Chronicles was first published in 2019, it was the culmination of many months of collecting stories and a Lifetime of Fishing. Seeing my stories in black and white, wrapped in the beautiful cover artwork of my friend R.J. Boyle, meant I had accomplished something that had been on my mind for along time. It was great fun creating the book and introducing it to a public eager to read what I had to say. I went on something of a book tour, or you might say I continued doing my usual seminars here and there, and used those opportunities to promote the book.

But as I thought about the book, something in my thoughts kept nagging me. I was happy with the selection of stories that I told, but then another story would come to mind, and I would regret that I forgot to tell it in the book. Darn, and that was a good story too. Then I had friends who came to me and said they had read my book, but what about this story or that one. I had left out so much and started making a list.

My writer and friend, Pat Mansell, accompanied me on a number of these seminar/book-signing events and I would tell him of these disturbing thoughts about my unfinished work. So after a few times of my mentioning it, Pat said I had better make a list so I wouldn't forget. That's what I did; I started making a list. Then one day I told him that I had a list of fourteen stories and several more in my head. He rolled his eyes and chuckled. "We'd better get busy," was all he said.

We both knew we were signing up for more work, but we also knew we were signing up for more fun. This gave me an opportunity to roll out a bunch more stories, some new fishing advice, recipes, and bring home my message of ocean conservation, respect for all God's creatures, and enthusiasm for the hook, line, and sinker. Many of the characters from the first book reappear here. And some new characters are introduced.

There is also a new feature to go along with this book that was not available when the original Chronicles was published. The website www.bouncersmithchronicles.com was created. This website is pictorial expression of many of the stories in the book. So, in addition to reading the words on the pages, my readers can also follow along online with some great photos. Here the experience is made much richer because you can read about a person, place, or fish, and you don't have to imagine it in your head, you can see it for yourself. I think this is a very unique approach to storytelling that amplifies the experience for the reader.

So I would call this new book more than an extension of the first book. It is that and more. So, dig in, get ready for an adventure in reading, and fire up the computer and log in. I think you'll find the experience different and rewarding. Thanks for tuning in and supporting me along the way.

Tight lines and Fish On.

Captain Bouncer Smith

The Long Ride From Andros

Ray Stormont was a member of the Miami Beach Rod and Reel Club and a really great angler. He hired me, along with Dixie Burns, to fish in a Miami Beach Rod and Reel Club competition in Fresh Creek, Andros. We had a good week of fishing and caught a bunch of big skipjack tunas, a bunch of bonefish, and we saw a lot of action.

One day we hired a guide to go bone fishing. We ran up Fresh Creek a ways and pulled over to a bank that was a beautiful bonefish flat. The guide said, "OK you guys get out and wade here. We're going to take the ladies somewhere else to fish." Buddy Yarborough was with us and he grabbed a handful of shrimp and stuck them in his shirt pocket. He took a couple of bucktails and stuck them in another shirt pocket. He grabbed his spinning rod and jumped overboard. Ray Stormont was going to fly fish, so he had his fly rod and reel and was wearing a fishing vest. He had to take off his upper left pocket and replace it with a different pocket. Then he took off the lower right pocket and replaced it with the one that used to be on the upper left – they were Velcroed in place. He put leader material in one pocket, and nippers on with a retractable coiler and attached that to a zipper in front. Then he made some other adjustments, and then changed from his

3

boat shoes to his wading boots. Next he had to change from his baseball style cap to his bonefish cap with the longer bill and the flap hanging down in the back. Then he changed from his gray sun shades to his copper sun shades so he could see on the flat better. After a lengthy preparation while we all sat around, he was finally ready to get out of the boat. Dixie said, "Wait a minute. Let me take your picture with all your garb." So she lined up the camera to take his picture, but before she did she said, "Ray, before I take this picture, I think you ought to zip up your fly."

So then they got out of the boat to bone fish, but didn't catch any. The girls and I and the guide went on up Fresh Creek, threw the big anchor over the side, tied it off and looked over. There was a huge school of bonefish and we caught about twenty-five of the little guys and had an absolute ball.

That's the fishing part of the story, now here's what this story is really about, the trip home. Dixie and Buddy flew home and Ray and I were taking the boat home, my 256 Dusky with twin outboards. Running up the coast of Andros the sea was right on the beam. Unfortunately it was blowing twenty-five to thirty out of the northeast. To give an idea of how rough it was, we were running along with a Bertram that was a boat nearly twice our size. It blew out a porthole and had to return to Fresh Creek. It couldn't take the waves pounding against its side and got knocked out of the game early. But we continued on. Ray and I were riding in the trough and holding on for dear life. There was no current there so the tide wasn't an issue.

Ray was my navigator, and as soon as we reached the end of Andros I asked, "Is it deep enough to go straight across from here, or do we have to go all the way up to the Northwest

Channel Light?" By going all the way up to the Northwest Channel Light we were going to have to continue taking this beating for many more miles.

Ray said, "No, I think we can make it straight across on the chart here. I see some channels we can follow."

So we took off across the north end of Andros Island. Whatever that chart said, it wasn't very reliable. It looked on the chart like there was enough water to run safely across the flats, but we had to run at least twenty or thirty miles with the engines trimmed up as far as we could have them at full speed, and with mud flying up behind the boat. We couldn't have been drawing more than a foot and half of water. It was so shallow that if there had been a conch shell sticking up on that bank it would have torn a hole in the bottom of the boat. It was pucker time the whole way, but we eventually made it across.

Then we got off the flats and onto the bank itself where the water was about ten feet deep. It was very choppy and we were taking spray constantly because of the angle we had to take. We were scheduled to pick up Dennis Forgione in Bimini where he had been with George Poveromo. His own boat was back in Miami, and he was going to ride back with us because he and I had to be in a Dusky Owners Tournament the following morning.

Ray and I had already taken a beating running in all this weather, skinny water, solid spray, medium chop, and ugly water. We got to Bimini and fueled up at the Big Game Club, and here came Dennis down the dock. He said, "We're not going to Miami in this weather are we?"

I said, "Sure we are. We're going right now."

Dennis said, "I'm not going to Miami in this weather. It's blowing thirty out of the northeast."

I said, "Well, I'm going."

He said, "Well, if you're going, I have to go."

I said, "Well, I'm going." We both had to be back because we were both sponsored by Dusky. "I'm leaving, Dennis, either get on or stay here."

"Well, if your going then I'm going." So Dennis grabbed his bag and jumped on the boat. We took off running across the Gulf Stream. And boy, I mean to tell you, it was stacked up. We had a northeast wind blowing thirty or better against the north current of the Gulf Stream. It was creating waves so big I would say to Ray, "How far is it down to the bottom of this wave?"

He'd say, "You don't want to know."

Then we'd be down in the trough and I'd say, "Just how high is this wave?"

He'd say, "It's higher than the outriggers."

The waves were at least twelve to fifteen feet. There might have been some twenty footers. Or it might have been the adrenaline and they were only ten to twelve feet, but either way it was really rough. We were making pretty good time, but unfortunately I finally got caught off guard and fell off the side of the top of one of these waves. We slid literally sideways down the face of the wave and slammed into the trough. All the coolers went flying; Dennis went flying. I ended up holding on to the steering wheel, but all the way over on the port side of the boat, and the steering wheel was on the starboard side. Ray was holding on to a rope that was secured to the t-top. He was between the cabin and the side of the boat hanging on for dear life.

We got everything squared away, tied the coolers down where they wouldn't move if they got tossed, and we got up and running again. Ray and I were standing behind the fish-

6

around cuddy cabin behind the windshield, and Dennis was sitting on the back seat. I was hearing some kind of noise, sounding like voices. I looked up and the VHF radio was turned off. I didn't have a stereo, but we were hearing this noise. I said, "Ray do you hear that?"

He said, "Yeah, I hear something."

I said, "What the heck is it?"

Ray turned around and bent over the back seat where Dennis was sitting and there he was saying Hail Marys, praying we would make it home. Dennis and I are the best of friends, and I know he's going to be mad about the story, but we got home and made it to the event the next day. It was so rough that nobody went fishing. We just had a big picnic and told fishing stories. We had a live band there and a big cook out. It was a Dusky Owners Dolphin Tournament and we had a great time. It was a harrowing trip home from Andros, but what a great trip it was.

167-Pound Alison Tuna on Twenty

Hans Demetz was a diamond broker from Holland who really changed my life. He called me up after taking delivery of a new boat, a 256 Dusky, right before Christmas in 1979. He wanted to know if I would run it whenever he wanted to go fishing. That sounded pretty good to me.

One day the wind was blowing out of the south. We had a hard time getting bait, but we got some big black mullet somewhere in our travels. We were down off South Beach and the water was dirty, ugly green. Nothing looked good for fishing, but I put two black mullet on a kite on twenty-pound test on custom-built rods. We were drifting in about 150 feet of water and there was no edge anywhere we could see. Nothing was happening until all of a sudden out of the water came this beautiful yellowfin tuna. I've never figured out whether there's a yellowfin tuna and an Alison tuna, or if an Alison tuna is a mature yellowfin tuna. But Alison tunas have long yellow streamers that come off their second dorsal fin all the way back to their tail, and off their anal fin all the way back to their tail: just absolutely beautiful streamer fins. But anyway, this big tuna came flying out of the water eating our mullet on the long kite. I was in total shock. I was winding to get tight on this fish, and here he came out of the water again and ate our short kite mullet.

Hans grabbed the other rod and got tight on his line. We had him on both rods when he took off on a blistering run. Now we had this big fish on. Hans was fighting it, and we knew we had him on both baits, so I was just kind of milking it along keeping the slack out of the second rod while Hans was doing all the hard work. I was just hoping this fish would stay on because boy, it was the catch of a lifetime, and was it ever beautiful. Hans was sweating and working, and I was just biding my time, keeping my line tight and bending my rod a little. I didn't want to get any slack in my line.

It was probably well over an hour that Hans fought this tuna. He got it up to the boat and I gaffed it, and the two of us pulled it into the boat. We were just overjoyed with this big old yellowfin or Alison tuna. We put it in the boat and went to Fred Lou Bait and Tackle in North Miami Beach. We weighed the tuna and it was 167 pounds; I'll never forget it.

But to see this fish skyrocket in the air with these bright yellow fins was just the most amazing thing. And to have it jump twice, and see it jump both times, it was just unbelievable. We all ate some yellowfin tuna out of that fish, I can tell you that.

Hans Demetz and I had a long history. He sold me his boat and we continued to fish. We went to Key West and fished, and we fished off Miami. And we fished out of Miami Beach Marina when I moved my boat down there. The last time we went fishing together we were tarpon fishing off South Beach. They weren't biting for a couple of hours and we didn't get a bite and I haven't seen Hans since. But I hope all is well with him and I really miss my days with Hans Demetz.

Costa Rica

Somewhere in the mid 2000s I decided to clean out my warehouse. Joe Singer agreed to sell all my accumulated stuff from the warehouse, and some of his stuff at the marine flea market. He was selling all my old decrepit fishing tackle and some of his as well. In the course of the weekend he raised several thousand dollars. My material and Joe's hard effort worked out really well. Joe could sell ice to an Eskimo; he was a really good salesman.

We had a nice pile of change left over so we decided the best way to use that money was to take a trip to Costa Rica to target roosterfish. It would be Joe and Sue and me, and I was put in charge of arranging it. So I called a travel agent called Fish South to arrange to not only fish in Costa Rica, but also to see some of the country. Unfortunately, before the trip came to fruition, Sue broke her leg severely while she and Joe were up in Canada. She was still on the mend when it was time to go to Costa Rica, so her son Keith, my nephew, joined our party. It was the three amigos, and it was a really great bonding trip.

The three amigos flew to San Jose, Costa Rica. We had arranged for a van to provide us transportation everywhere we went. The driver met us at the airport and loaded up our luggage. We got in the van and headed up through the mountains to a rainforest. Joe was a fisherman, a boat racer, a car racer, an auto mechanic, a mechanical engineer, and he designed rocket ship parts. He was an all around man's man. He could fix absolutely anything, and he loved fishing and could do all kinds of outdoor sports.

Here we were traveling through the mountains of Costa Rica in this van, and Joe got carsick. We were driving through the mountains while Joe was puking out the window of the van. We got to the rainforest and the nice little lodge we were booked into. We had arranged to go white water rafting while we were there, so the rafting company picked us up in the morning and drove us up the river a ways. We got to a bridge over the river where we met our guide and our camera crew and our lifeguard. We had a big rubber raft and a couple of kayaks, and we headed down the river. It was fantastic! Beautiful scenery and birds, and white water and calm water. You never knew where to look next.

As we were going down the river we were all getting soaked with spray. We actually had lifeguards with us in separate kayaks so if anybody went overboard they could rescue him and bring him back to the raft. And don't you know it, we were going down one set of rapids and were doing a big whoop-di-do hump, and Joe went flying out of the raft. The lifeguard had to rescue him and bring him back to the raft.

We went on down the river and came to a spot where we could jump in and swim. Then we went down a little further and beached the raft and snacked on fresh fruit. Then we got back in the raft and headed a little further down and got to the end of our ride. The van was waiting for us and we got in and went to a restaurant where they gave us a beautiful lunch. They gave us a CD of all of the pictures of our trip and we asked for extra CDs since they were so inexpensive.

11

I asked the guide, what should I tip each of the guys? He said that twenty dollars was more than enough. So I gave each of the five guys who were with us twenty dollars. The guide said, "Oh no, I meant twenty dollars for all of us."

I said, "That's all right. You guys really earned it. You had to rescue Joe from drowning you know."

We went back to the rainforest and the next morning the van picked us up and took us to Arenal Lodge to look at the Arenal Volcano. We got there and checked into the hotel and went to our rooms. Joe went out on the balcony of his room to check out the scenery and a giant macaw attacked him. I don't know if he spooked the macaw or what, but they collided. Joe was all flustered and it was a crazy event.

It was hazy and rainy and we couldn't see the mountain, so Keith and I went down to the bar to shoot pool, and for the first time in my life I was drinking Black Russians. Joe came down to join us and we were all sitting there at the bar and playing pool. At about 4:30 in the afternoon Joe looked out of the window and said, "Bouncer, look at that!" I turned around and there was a clear view of the volcano.

So we quit shooting pool and grabbed three Cuban cigars and three Black Russians and sat out on the patio and watched the volcano erupting. We watched it right on through sundown and into dark. We could see the lava flows, and it was a really spectacular volcano display that lasted for four hours. After four hours of the three of us and everybody else in the hotel watching this volcano action the maître 'd of the restaurant came out and said, "I hate to spoil your fun, but the kitchen closes at nine o'clock and it's eight thirty now. If you don't order you won't get any dinner."

Everybody went inside and started ordering dinner, and don't you know it, ten minutes later it started pouring down rain. We stayed there all the next morning and left about eleven o'clock and never saw the mountain again. We had a four hour special showing, a beautiful dinner, another abuse of Joe, and the van driver picked us up to take us to a coffee plantation.

Driving down the road we saw a whole family of ring-tailed lemurs. We saw some other wildlife at the volcano lodge. We went on up to the plantation and checked into our hotel there. At the plantation we learned all about the making of coffee.

The following day the van picked us up and took us back to San Jose. From there we took an airplane down to Golfito where we met Bobby McGuiness for three days of fishing. We explained that our number one goal was to catch roosterfish. The first day we went out and caught a bunch of blue runners. We fished numerous near shore rock formations and caught a whole lot of roosterfish on bait and on jigs. I also caught a big jack crevalle and it was a wonderful day.

Our deal with Keith was that if we caught a bunch of roosterfish, then he could try to catch a marlin. We told Bobby that we wanted to go rooster fishing in the morning when they bit the best, and then we'd go fishing for marlin in the afternoon. Bobby suggested it would be better if we marlin fished in the morning.

The next morning we got up and ran a long, long way to a seamount. We put out lures to catch small tunas for live bait. But we had no luck getting a bite with that. So we put out a trolling spread, which included a rigged bonito, and started trolling around. Well, it wasn't long before a nice 400-pound blue marlin ate the rigged bonito, and Keith was in business. Lots of fighting, lots of beautiful jumps, and he got the fish to the boat one time. The mate had to let go of the leader because it was too wild. Then the fish got tail wrapped.

On the way to the fishing grounds I had pointed out in the tackle box that there was a tuna tamer. This is a cylindrical led device that slides down the main line. It has eight fingers that stick out to catch the snap swivel as it is pulled back up. Then the angler has two outfits with which to pull the fish to the surface. The marlin had gotten tail wrapped and gone down deep and stopped fighting. This way the marlin was going to die down there and it was going to take hours to get it up. So I told the mate to get the tuna tamer, drop it down, and Keith and I could both pull the fish up to the boat. So that's what we did. We dropped the tuna tamer and it caught the snap swivel. Keith would pull up and wind down; I would pull up and he would wind down, and in a short time we had a very tired marlin up to the boat. I unwrapped his tail and moved the boat forward and got him swimming again and sent him on his way.

After that we ran inshore and Joe hooked a tuna but, unfortunately, it came off. Then we got to the rocks and I caught a couple of small fish, and Keith caught a couple of small fish, but Joe didn't catch a fish all day.

So let me get this straight now, Joe got carsick, Joe fell out of the raft white water rafting, Joe got clocked by the macaw, and Joe was the only one who got skunked while we were fishing. I think Joe had a monkey on his back.

The next day we ran almost to Panama and caught world record mullet snappers on fly. I realized my number one goal of the trip, which was to catch a roosterfish on a surface popper. We caught bluefin trevallies; it was just another great day of fishing. We went back and had mullet snapper cooked up for dinner at a restaurant, and the next day flew back to San Jose and then back to Miami.

What a great bonding trip for Keith and Joe and me in Costa Rica. It was really a super good trip.

Father Chris Marino

I was over in Bimini with Dixie Burns and Ray Stormont, and we had a good day of fishing. We were tied up at the Bimini Big Game Club. I was cleaning fish and my mate was cleaning up the boat, and a young man walked up and started shooting the breeze with me. In a few minutes he introduced himself as Father Chris, and he had been told by Captain Jack Plachter that if I should show up in the Bahamas he should introduce himself. In the cockpit with me was Dixie Burns, a long time customer. So Father Chris and I shot the breeze about the fishing he had done and his adventures with Jack Plachter, and how he was there to perform the Sunday services at the Catholic Church in Bimini.

After a long and pleasant conversation, Dixie grabbed my left shirtsleeve and pulled on it a little bit. I turned around and she whispered over, "Are Catholic priests allowed to go out to dinner?"

I said to Dixie, "I don't know." I turned to Father Chris and asked, "Father Chris, would you like to join us for dinner?"

He said, "Oh, that would be so wonderful. Thank you."

So we cleaned up a bunch of fish and took it to the kitchen at the Big Game Club, and went to our rooms to clean up. We came back and sat down to a fantastic fish dinner with all the trimmings. Father Chris sat on one side of me and Dixie sat on the other side, and we went on with great conversation. As dinner was coming to an end Dixie pulled on my sleeve again. I turned around and she whispered, "Are priests allowed to go fishing?"

I turned to Father Chris and asked, "Is there any chance you could go fishing with us tomorrow?"

He said, "Oh, I'd love to."

So Father Chris went with us the next day. We went to a wreck up in the gulf. The highlight of the day for Dixie was when she was throwing a Bomber Long A with three treble hooks and caught three yellowtail snappers at the same time. When she lifted them into the boat she was all aglee and was shouting, "This was the holy trinity of yellowtails. It could happen only with Father Chris on the boat."

We went on to catch snappers and groupers, and all kinds of good fish that day. We went back and cleaned some up for Father Chris, and the rest for ourselves. It was a great trip to the Bahamas as Father Chris excused himself to perform church services over the weekend.

A year later we were going back to Bimini and Dixie insisted that Father Chris be part of our troop. So we had Dixie Burns, and Ray Stormont, and Buddy Yarborough, and Father Chris as we went over to the Bahamas. We got over there and anchored up, and were catching nice yellowtails, a pound and a half to two pounds. Something started to eat our yellowtails, which happens a lot over there, so Ray asked to have a thirty-pound outfit to fish a live yellowtail for bait to see what he could catch. So Ray floated out a yellowtail, and in short order it got eaten, but whatever ate it ran into the bottom and got away. So Ray rigged up again. Unfortunately, when the predators start eating the yellowtails, the yellowtails stop biting. It became very hard to catch one, and each time we caught one we put on Ray's line, but every one he floated out would be lost to the critters.

Father Chris was becoming upset because everyone knows yellowtails are a fantastic to eat, and Ray was using them all for bait. Shortly thereafter Father Chris caught a yellowtail about three and a half pounds. He grabbed that yellowtail and ripped the gills out and ran up and threw it in the fish box, and said, "You're not going to use that one for bait." He even threw in some mild cuss words at that point. But he warned us that if we continued to abuse his yellowtails that the language was going to get much, much worse.

We've had a great relationship with Father Chris. Unfortunately, a short time thereafter I lost my son. Not having a religious connection to call upon, I asked Father Chris if he would perform the services for my son. He agreed and did a great job of it.

A couple of years later we had to call on Father Chris again to perform the services for my brother-in-law, Joe, when he passed away. In between we still fished with Father Chris occasionally. Now I try to get him out at least once a year to go fishing for his enjoyment and to stock his freezer so he could have a few good fresh fish dinners.

What a blessing it has been to have Father Chris in our lives. We had him out just last week and caught a bunch of yellow-eye snappers and squirrelfish, which he was sure his parishioners would eat. But then when he had to scale them it became quite the chore as squirrelfish are covered with sharp scales and sharp spines.

Thank you Father Chris for all you have done for my family.

Dolphin Francaise

There's a pub in Dania, Florida, that I simply love to visit. Its name is Shenanigans. It's a sports bar, it's a pub, and it's a great restaurant. The ambiance is very casual with interesting memorabilia, a dozen or more TV screens showing sports events, and a great place to people watch. A fishing club that I am very close to meets there once a month. Many of the club members are among my best friends, and the food is fantastic. A night at Shenanigans is simply the best.

The menu goes from fish, to burgers, to chicken, salads, ribs, and steaks. It is impossible to get a bad meal there. The wait staff is friendly and patient, and the Chef is a real pro. Speaking of the Chef, one of his signature dishes, one that will blow your mind, is called Dolphin Francaise, and here's how he tells us it's made:

Put dolphin fillets in flour and thoroughly coat them before shaking off the excess flour. That way when the filets go into an egg batter, the batter adheres to the fish. The fillets then go into a pan with hot oil and Chef gently shakes the pan to keep the fish from sticking. When a well-defined crust forms at the edges of the filets, turn the fish over with tongs to cook the other side, again shaking the pan so the oil coats the fish. After a couple of minutes in the pan, put the golden brown filets into another pan with some of the hot oil and put that pan in the oven. Then drain the excess oil from the original pan and glaze the pan with white wine. Reduce it for a minute or two with some chicken stock and fresh pieces of lemon. The next step is to add pieces of buerre manie, which is a fifty/fifty mix of flour and butter kneaded together in small cubes.

"It's an uncooked roux," says Chef of the buerre manie. "When you put it in, that gets the sauce right off the bat. If you

18

keep it small like this as you add it to the sauce, it'll boil and cool." By keeping the fillets in a separate pan, the batter doesn't come off the fish. After adding some fresh chopped parsley to the sauce and some more buerre manie, Chef puts the fillets in the pan with the sauce, then plates them and drizzles the sauce on the side. The result is indescribably delicious.

Tom Hobbs

I can't for the life of me figure out how this story didn't make book one. When we moved from Michigan in 1956 I was in the sixth grade and went to Norland Elementary School. In that grade our class had Phys Ed for an hour and we often played volleyball. I was the world's worst athlete all through school. One time I was on the left sideline and the ball came to me, deflected off my hands and went off across the basketball court. I went to retrieve the volleyball and was bringing it back, crossing the basketball court, doing my rendition of dribbling. So I was bouncing the volleyball across the basketball court taking my own good time. The school jock, Tom Hobbs, who really was the school jock (he would run around the halls in the schools singing, "I'm Johnny Unitas. His sidekick, John Kirkland would be hollering, "I'm Lenny Moore.")

So Tom Hobbs hollered over, "OK, Bouncer, quit bouncing the ball around. We only have a little time to play here." From then on I was stuck with the name Bouncer. Every class year I went to school with the same kids, and in every class when the teacher would do roll call on the first day of the year, they would call out, "Randolph Smith."

I would say, "That's me, but my family calls me Randy."

And somebody in the class would chime in, "Yeah, but you're Bouncer around here."

When I left high school I decided that was it. I was leaving Bouncer at the front door, and I again became Randy Smith. In very short order I got a job on the *Top Luck* at the Castaways Motel. I was Randy Smith and my boss' name was Randy Lacey. Randy Lacy Jr. worked a mile down the beach, and he stopped by every morning and every afternoon. And Randy Lacey III would come fishing on the weekends. And lo and behold, I hired a mate whose name was Randy Keith. The mate on the boat next door was Randy Travis. It was just solid Randys as far as the eye could see.

I said, "That's it. I was Bouncer all through school, I'm going back to being Bouncer." So Bouncer Smith became the professional fisherman, and the name has treated me like a king my whole life.

After years of enjoying and taking advantage of the unusual the name I got a phone call from a judge in Texas and he said, "Hey, this is Tom Hobbs. I'm coming to Florida for the class reunion and I figure I ought to go fishing with you. I see so much about your fishing."

I said, "That would be great."

So I took Tom Hobbs, who gave me my name, out fishing several times. We were out there fishing one day and my mate, Abie Raymond, was in the back of the boat with Tom Hobbs while I was driving. Tom said to Abie, "You know, that Bouncer, he screwed up a good thing for me."

Abie asked, "How did he do that?"

Tom replied, "I have to admit that I was not only the school jock, but I guess I was a bit of a bully. When I called him Bouncer it was intended as derogatory, but look what that guy has done with what I did to him. He's an all right guy. Ain't it great to live in America."

21

Go With the Flow

Here's a tip that can work out on a lot of different applications – it's called Go With The Flow. As we fish in saltwater, and sometimes even in fresh water, we have to see which way the water flows because it will tell us which way the bait will travel. The predator fish recognize the proper travels of the baitfish. The first example is fishing in the inlet for snook, tarpon, jacks, and permit. On an incoming tide the water goes from the ocean to the bay, and on an outgoing tide it goes from the bay to the ocean. So, if we're targeting snook on the outgoing tide, and we drift with the tide, our baits will be swimming along with the current much like the baitfish will be moving with the tide in nature. A three or four inch shrimp can't swim upstream against a two knot current. Therefore that shrimp is naturally going to be going down tide, with the tide. The same thing happens with a two-inch pilchard. A pilchard may go upstream for a few minutes, but when all is said and done, that pilchard is going to be pushed out with the tide. Therefore when you're targeting fish like snook, mangrove snappers, even tarpon, and if you're fishing in an inlet, you want to run up tide and drift down tide with the current.

You can anchor and hold your baits in the current. That would be an acceptable presentation to some extent because fish like finger mullet and pinfish get down on the bottom, and will be able to hold themselves against the current. They won't be able to swim against the current, but they will be able to hold the bottom much like if you anchor and fish on the bottom with a sinker. All in all, the best presentation if you're in that inlet is if your bait is moving with the tide at about the same speed as the tide. The snook, the grouper, the tarpon, the mangrove snapper, whatever it is, he's going to be facing up tide watching for this bait to be carried down tide to feed him. It's a natural feeding station where the baitfish are coming with the tide to the predator fish that are holding against the current. It's much easier for a thirty-inch snook to hold against the current than it is for a three-inch shrimp. So when you're fishing in an inlet, it may be more work, but go up tide and drift down with the current and fish your baits at the water level of the targeted species. If you're looking for snook, you're going to want those baits down near the bottom. For permit your baits should be on the surface or in midlevel. Tarpon will be at midlevel or on the surface as well because that's where their baitfish are most likely to come through.

The exact same rules apply when fishing along a beach. If you go off as an example, South Beach (Miami Beach) there are swim buoys along there. If you pull up to a swim buoy or two you can usually see the current pushing against them. A lot of times, in the case of South Beach, that current will be going toward the south. If you have a light south current, and the wind is blowing from the south to the north, which is called a south wind, they are opposed to each other. If you're fishing live shrimp and there's a strong south wind pushing you to the north, and a light south current trying to push bait to the south, your boat is going to drag your baits against the current which results in an unnatural presentation. If the tarpon are hungry enough you'll still do OK, but if they're borderline, then you really want your shrimp to be traveling with the current.

A prime example of what happens here is, one day a couple of years ago we had a guy on the boat who really liked to cast and retrieve. So we were fishing three live shrimp on flat lines with small split shots, but they were drifting with the wind. The boat was moving slowly to the north while the current was moving slowly to the south. To counter balance this incorrect motion of the bait I gave my angler a weighted hook with a live shrimp on it. He would cast to the north and wind back to the south just like the current was running. In short order he hooked three tarpon on the cast-and-retrieve shrimp going with the current, while the three baits going slowly against the current never got a bite.

In the natural progression of things, you want to go with the flow. If the baitfish are moving from north to south in nature, you want your bait to move from north to south. If the wind is stronger than the current, then your baits are going in the wrong direction, and unless the fish are really hungry you may not get a bite.

Probably my most notable success with 'go with the flow' was when we were fishing the very last Miami Billfish Tournament. On the first day of the two day tournament the wind was pretty strong out of the southeast. It seems everybody in the fleet was kite fishing. The current was going to the north, and there was a southeast wind that was pushing the boats to the north. Everybody, ourselves included, had pretty good fishing. We managed to do well enough that we were in the hunt all through the day, and we were in the top ten at the end of the first day. We all went out fishing the second day and the current was still running to the north fairly well, but the wind out of the south had almost completely quit.

So everybody put up their kites with helium balloons. To keep the kites at an angle out behind the boat, and keep the baits hanging straight back and not right on top of the boat, everybody was bumping their boats forward, ourselves included. So we were all fighting the current and nobody was getting any bites. I finally told Abie, "We have got to stop fighting the current. We're just going to let her drift."

So we loaded up on the flat lines. The kite was pretty much straight up and down for a little while, and as we drifted by the Miami Sea Buoy, we caught a couple of sailfish. After we got a little ways past the buoy, and we didn't get any more bites, we ran back south of the buoy again, and once again we drifted right through the middle of the fleet. Everybody was bumping their boats to the south while we were drifting to the north. We caught a couple of more sailfish while everybody else watched and scratched their heads. So I ran back to the south again and we did it again. In the course of the day we caught five or six sailfish right in the middle of all the traffic. We were going north with the current while they were standing still or going south against the current and having little or no luck. So this was another case where going with the flow made all the difference in the world. I can't over emphasize, in all your fishing, when all else fails, 'go with the flow'. It can really make a difference.

Now, to give credit where credit is due, how I did so well in that tournament was from a lesson I learned in a Bob Lewis Billfish Tournament years ago. The wind was blowing twenty-five to thirty out of the north, and the current was going to the north. I was in a Dusky 256, and all the other boats in the tournament were fifty and sixty foot sportfishing boats. Being so rough, the best approach we could make would be to drift with the kite up and some flat lines out, and just let

25

the wind take us against the current. We weren't seeing any sailfish. The bigger boats drove into the wind with the current to keep their kites out behind their boats, and they were consistently hooking up. As the day progressed and I hadn't learned my lesson about going with the flow yet, I finally said that all these boats that were going with the current were catching fish, but the wind was holding us back against the current, and we weren't getting any shots. So I finally started driving against the wind, which made for a very difficult presentation for us on account of the strong wind against the small boat. But we did drive against the wind a little bit and we finally started to see some sailfish. That's where I first learned how important it is to go with the flow when you're live baiting.

People ask me, "Why doesn't this apply to trolling?" If your current is running two knots to the north, and you troll straight north at six knots, you're going over the fish at eight knots. Bear in mind that the current at the surface is going two knots, but only extends ten or fifteen feet below the surface. A fish that is fifteen feet down is actually not fighting the current that the boat is. If the bait goes by at eight knots, it is not very appealing to the fish. If they're facing south, your bait goes flying by to the north and just blows by. If you're trolling south at four knots and the current is going north at two knots, at least your bait is just barely just making headway, and it's offering a presentation to the fish.

So those are some thoughts on 'go with the flow' that can apply in any situation. It can be trout fishing in a mountain stream — you'll never see a dry fly swimming up against the current. It can apply fishing a mangrove point in the Everglades. A snook will be hiding behind that mangrove branch, and he expects that pilchard, or shrimp, or finger mullet to be coming out with the tide to where he can ambush it. He never expects a baitfish to swim up behind him because it would be unnatural for the baitfish to go against the current and sneak past the forty-five inch snook. That just wouldn't happen. And of course if anything happens with a bonefish on a grass flat or a mangrove snapper on a wreck, whatever it is, if you can't get a bite, try going with the flow. It can make all the difference. Good luck.

Andre's Ceviche

Being out in the boat for a day of fishing creates the perfect opportunity to use some of that freshly caught fish you just threw on the ice. You may or may not have cooking facilities on your boat, but with ceviche you do not need a flame. The citrus juice from lemons and oranges does the cooking for you, and boy, are the results ever great. Here's how it's done:

Cut up an onion, red pepper, scallions, cilantro, and garlic. Add in red wine vinegar, olive oil, the juice of six limes, the juice of two or three oranges, and the juice of one lemon. The choice of fish is yours, but Andre recommends triggerfish, tuna, wahoo, grouper, or tilefish. Cut your fish into cubes ¼ to ½ inches.

Mix the ingredients in a bowl. The citrus juice must reach the top of the solid ingredients. The longer it sits, the better, at least an hour. Mix again before serving. Prepare for a real treat because this recipe is going to make your day.

Oregon Inlet, NC

In the early 1970s I was between boats. Pflueger Taxidermy wanted to sent someone up to Oregon Inlet, just south of Nags Head, North Carolina, to keep them in a good light with the charter boat fleet there. So they allowed me to be their representative up there. I had a pickup truck with a bed cover, so I set it up with a mattress and enough accessories that I could live in my truck for a couple of months. It certainly wasn't prime living, but it got the job done. I was young and dumb and tough. If you're going to be dumb, you've got to be tough you know.

At any rate, I drove up to Oregon Inlet and started hanging around the docks. With the connections of Jerry and Jesse Webb of Pflueger I was invited to fish on a few boats. I'm not certain of the name of the first captain who had me on his boat, but I believe it might have been Tillett, which is a common name up there. We started off where our trips were predominantly trolling for kingfish, and I learned something very quick there. They trolled four planers, two on rods and reels, and two on hand lines. The hand lines were tied off the stern cleats using bungee cords for a shocker. They would have a customer standing there with gloves on, and when it got hit the customer would hand line in this planer, put the planer in the boat, hand line in the kingfish, and flip him into the boat.

28

If a kingfish hit the planers on the rods and reels, the customer would reel it in, and the customer with the gloves on would hand line it in the rest of the way and swing it into the boat. This went on pretty much all day.

It got more exciting one afternoon when we hit into a school of bluefin tunas. We caught several thirty to fifty pound bluefins. But it was one of the low points of my life when I went to unload one of the tunas onto the dock and dropped it into the ocean. A fifty-pound bluefin tuna down into the depths of the Oregon Inlet Harbor. We couldn't see through the surface of the water; that tuna was lost and gone forever. Boy did I get some ugly looks from the captain, the mate, and the anglers when that happened, but in the end they forgave me.

One of my favorite memories of Oregon Inlet was that when we backed into the dock, we put on the lines and unloaded our catch into wheelbarrows. When the fish attendant pulled up with that wheelbarrow he'd unload a giant ice-cold watermelon on to the cutting table next to the boat. Then he would load all the fish into the wheelbarrow and give the customers a number. The attendant would roll the wheelbarrow away and take it into the fish house. The fish house was attached to a sit down, screened in restaurant and refreshment stand. The customers would bid their adieu to the crew and go into the restaurant for a few beers or iced tea, or whatever. They might order a fish sandwich, or hamburger, or French fries, and in a little while their number would be called. They would go up to a counter and be informed that they had 220 pounds of fish, and it was ten cents or twenty cents a pound to process. They would pay the money and get all their fish all fileted up, boned out, packaged up, and on ice ready to go to take home. It was quite an operation.

29

As a crew member on the boat, when the boat was tied up, we'd unload the fish and rinse out the cockpit. The captains and mates gathered around this giant, ice-cold watermelon and devoured it as they compared fish stories from the day. When the watermelon was pretty much gone, the crew would jump on the boat and soap it down and get it ready for the next day. After the boat was clean, they would settle down at the rigging table on the dock and rig up baits for the next day, giant squids, horse ballyhoo, mackerel, if they were going offshore; bonito strips, swimming mullet, or kingfish bellies if they were going to fish for kingfish.

An interesting trick they did with their kingfish is they would troll planers with three and a half and four drone spoons, but unlike I have ever seen in South Florida, they'd put in a quarter inch, by quarter inch, by two inch kingfish belly on the hook of the drone spoon. They felt that every time they put it out it put a little bit of scent in the water that really inspired those kings to bite the spoon. I've never seen it done in South Florida that way.

When we got to go fishing a bit further offshore, we hit beautiful blue water with weed lines and the potential for blue marlin, white marlin, yellowfin tuna, dolphin, and wahoo. It was quite a place to fish. I actually did more blue water fishing when I moved over to fish with Mike Merritt on the *Billfisher*.

When I was with Captain Tillett we were on the west side of the marina so our bow faced to the east. Now with Mike we were on the east side of the marina with the bow facing west. We had to keep the salon doors closed because we had a day boat with an open back and the windshield faced into the setting sun. For some reason every flying insect from the outer banks followed the sun in the afternoon. They would fly into our open-backed salon and just about black out the windshield as they tried to follow the sun. And our windshield didn't open, so we would have tons of dead flies eventually laying on our front dash. This had to be cleaned up every morning when we got to the boat.

What an honor it was to fish with Mike Merritt. Funny enough, last year I read a biography of him in one of the fishing magazines. It said he started his business three years after I worked for him. So somebody got their calendar messed up, because I know I was there in 1973, maybe 1974, and they talked about him starting his business in 1976. I had to get a chuckle out of that.

All these guys in the Oregon Inlet Fishing Center had big single diesels in these beautiful back yard-built sportfishing boats. They were beautiful with wide Carolina flairs, with beautiful layouts and woodwork, and they were fast as all get out. But they all had single engines. They would come into the Fishing Center, which was a full horseshoe layout, spin their boats around, and back them into their slips without issue.

I'll never forget, there were always a few hot dogs in the crowd. I remember when one of them came into the marina, spun around, just about got lined up with his slip, slammed it into reverse knowing exactly what he was going to do, and his shift cable broke with the engine running at high RPMs. He could pull back on the throttle, but he couldn't shift out of gear, and he had already built up the momentum. He backed into the piling; the piling flexed and sprung him half way across the marina. An embarrassing moment for that captain with a hundred people standing behind his slip to see his catch. It's better that he hit that flexible piling instead of making his mark in the slip and crashing into the bulkhead. The bulkhead would have no give and might have wrecked his boat and injured people on the dock.

31

So every night it was dinner at the Oregon Inlet Fishing Center Restaurant, pile into my truck, drive along the beautiful coast, drive around Nags Head a little bit and then over the causeway to Manteo, into the campground. I'd park my truck, crawl into my tailgate, and call it a night. After those long days on the water, and early rises the next day, I never had any problem getting a night's sleep.

Wes and Weasel Windless

Back in the early 70s I had been working on charter boats at the Castaways for several years. My wash down boy, Neal Orange, had gotten into working for Rider Yachts and on private boats. I was ready to move on to something new so I joined their efforts and started working at Ryder Yachts, which was a Hatteras dealership. The Ryder family was famous in the sailing world. And then I worked on a private boat, the *Sly Mongoose*, with Neal. We had some good times together.

I remember one time Wes Puller and I went out by the Miami Sea Buoy and we had a string of little baby jigs out to catch baby bonitos for bait. We had a whole string of baby bonitos on the line, and Wes unhooked one and put it on a hook and threw it out on an outrigger. It came charging back, and ended up swimming right up the exhaust pipe with a blue marlin hot on its tail. When the marlin understood that the bonito was out of reach he turned around and jumped on the other two bonitos hanging on the bait catching rig. That rig was made up of twelve pound test and little jigs with about number eight hooks. I guess he got wrapped up in it because that marlin was jumping all over the water, only hooked on twelve pound test and number eight hooks. There was no hope there, but it was a wild few minutes and he put on a great show. That was a very frustrating day as we went on to miss several white marlin off South Beach, but it was sure exciting while it lasted albeit a rough day both for the seas and the catch results.

Wes Puller, we just called Wes, and Neal Orange we named the Weasel. The three of us ended up in Bimini with John Graves where I was teaching them how to marlin fish. The fishing was very slow so I would sit up on the bridge and holler down, "Hey, there's a blue marlin after the left long." John would run over to the rod. I would tell him that the marlin was trying to eat it and to drop back. John would drop back. I would tell him to lock up and wind and he would do that. Of course it was all just a drill.

We were going to go home, so we were trolling down the edge and I was sicker than a dog. Neal was up on the bridge where I was lying down, and Wes and John were in the cockpit. After lying there for a while we had made our way down to Gun Cay so I sat up to see where we were. The line from the left outrigger went from the reel up to the outrigger release clip, and from there to a flat line mackerel on the right flat line. That would only happen if somehow they had gotten tangled together or something had eaten the outrigger bait and swam over to eat the mackerel. I started hollering, "Left rigger, left rigger."

John and Wes looked at me as if to say, "We've had that game before. We're not playing it anymore."

They were completely unresponsive until I started charging down the ladder. Then John grabbed the rod for the left outrigger, and as he wound tight, the line went under the mackerel. He came tight on a fish, so I let the mackerel further back to clear the line out of his way. I handed that rod to Wes over the top of John's. Now Wes had the mackerel and something started jerking on it so he gave it some line and hooked a fish. John and Wes each had fish on while I cleared the other lines. Somebody's fish was jumping parallel to the boat. It would jump and I would holler, "It's a white!" At least it was the right size for a white marlin. It would jump again and I would holler, "No, it's a blue!" because it had all the fins of a blue marlin. "It's a white, no, it's blue." Well, it was a marlin anyhow.

It turned out we had two fish on, and Wes got his up to the boat first. Back then, anything we wanted to have mounted had to be harvested and there were no size limits. Wes definitely wanted to mount his blue marlin so I gaffed it and was pulling it in the boat. Somehow the lazarette door had ben opened, maybe to get out a Billy club or a rope or something. But the bottom line was that John went to run across the back of the boat and he fell into the lazarette. His foot came down on the point of a grapple anchor and he received a severe injury on the bottom of his foot. But he got up out of there and it turned out he had a blue marlin as well. We boated this one too and headed back home. We had an eighty-seven pound blue marlin for Wes, and a 123 pound blue marlin for John, and it all started off with them thinking it was a hoax.

Probably my most memorable thought about Wes Puller and Neal Orange, the Weasel, was that on many occasions we anchored both off the Bahamas and off South Florida. The only way to get the anchor up on the *Sly Mongoose* was to pull it up by hand. This was back before the days of anchor balls, and I adopted the name the 'Wes and Weasel Windless' for whenever we had to pull the anchor. Even today, to get a chuckle out of Neal just mention the Wes and Weasel Windless.

Unfortunately Wes has gone to the big fishing grounds in the sky but he left behind two famous fishermen in Mike

Puller, and his son John. Mike runs his own charter boat, the *Lisa L* out of Crandon Park Marina. That boat was Wes' at one time, and then it was Mike's boat, and now it's Jim Puller's boat. Mike Puller, Wes' other son, runs private boats all around south Florida. All the Puller family made great names for themselves through fishing. And boy, Wes, and Weasel, and I had some great times together.

When Barracuda Attack

Everybody always talks about shark attacks, but sharks never jump in the boat to attack people. Barracudas are far more dangerous when it comes to attacks on people on their boats. There was the story about the woman who was hit in the throat by a barracuda that jumped in the boat. Fortunately its mouth was closed. There are stories of barracudas biting divers' hands when they were rubbing the side of the boat with a rag in their hand. There was a guide who was washing the side of his flats skiff and was flashing a towel back and forth and got bitten on the hand by a barracuda.

But how about the barracudas that attack people inside the boat? It would be logical that if you tried to pick one up wrong and got bit, but that's not what I'm talking about. One day we were fishing in Dumfoundling Bay in the very north end of Dade County. I had three guys fishing on my twenty-seven foot boat that day, and the guy in the middle was right in front of the console by the side of the boat. We were targeting tarpon with artificial lures, but would catch the occasional jack crevalle. One of the guys was throwing a very popular lure called the Zara Spook. It's a surface plug that does what they call 'walk the dog.' When we fish it we move it very fast with twitches of the rod and make it zigzag left and right. A big barracuda that turned out to be twenty-seven pounds grabbed the Zara Spook and raced around in a big circle. All of a sudden here came this barracuda flying out of the water aimed right at the guy. He dived out of the way and the barracuda crashed into the side of my console. The console was probably about three quarters of an inch thick solid fiberglass with a jell coat covering on it, and the barracuda hit it so hard that you would have thought it was hit with a sledge hammer. It left an imprint about the size of a baseball, and the jell coat and fiberglass were actually fractured. Thank goodness the guy jumped out of the way. The barracuda actually finished itself off, and the fellow had a mount made of it. That was a very scary event.

We have a great operation here in South Florida that was started by R.J. Boyle Studios in Pompano. R.J. started a program called Mission Fishin. They take handicapped children and their families out boating and fishing for a half a day on a Saturday. They started off with a couple of boats and it became very successful, so they put out the call on the Internet to the neighborhoods and asked for boats to volunteer. They connected up with a cerebral palsy group and they take these families out on the volunteers' boats. People volunteer to buy drinks and snacks and stuff, and the kids get on the boats and go out. They've had some very successful trips. I remember one time they had windy weather so they stayed in the inshore waters between Hillsboro and Boca Raton. Trolling rigged ballyhoo they caught barracudas, and mutton snappers, and bluefish, and snook.

I had a much scarier event happen here just a few months ago. We finally arranged for Mission Fishin to come to Miami Beach. We had several boats volunteered and several great families to join them. The family we took out was a mom and dad, the sick child, and two siblings. We were out in about twenty-five feet of water on a rock pile. The kids were catching baby yellowtails and grunts. Suddenly a barracuda came up to check out what we were up to. The next yellowtail we caught Abie put on a wire leader and cast it off the side of the boat. Sure enough the barracuda latched onto the yellowtail and hooked up. One of the siblings took the rod. The barracuda went in a big semi circle and came flying out of the water and slammed down right on top of our engines, then onto our dive platform, and then back into the ocean. If that barracuda had launched itself four feet later it would have crashed right into the cockpit where the challenged child and the mother were sitting on the back bench with their legs stretched out on the back deck, right where the barracuda would have landed with its one inch razor sharp teeth. If it landed a little off center it would have landed on one of the other two brothers. At any rate, just a little bit different aim and this barracuda could have created a real tragedy.

We have seen so many ten and fifteen and even twenty pound fish cut right in half with one bite of a barracuda, so we don't want to see any of our guests with that kind of bite on their body from these flying barracuda. It goes to show you to remain alert when you're out there fishing.

Slimy Catfish

I had a wonderful customer for years by the name of Gary Leff. He had four sons and they did a lot of fishing with me in Miami. Because there were four sons and Gary, there were too many people for me to take on my twenty-five foot Dusky. I would meet them at Haulover at about eight o'clock in the morning and three of them would get on the boat and we would go fishing. After a half-day we would return to Haulover and maybe two or three would get off and the others would get on. There might be a few others who would get on with them. Bill McClendon comes to mind as possibly being in the mix as well. Then we would go on an afternoon half-day trip. We would return to Haulover and some would get off, and some would get on, and we would go evening tarpon fishing for a couple of hours. We would do this for three or four days in a row, fourteen hours of fishing. A whole bunch of different people fishing outside of Haulover, and up and down the beach, fishing for barracuda and offshore for dolphin, and whatever the case may be. Gary and I built some great memories together.

Gary also had a condo in Panama City Beach in the panhandle. He invited my wife, Ruth, and my son, Terry, and me up to join him there. His boat was a nineteen-foot Boston Whaler. We would fill the boat with Gary and a couple of his sons, and Terry, and me, and we would go to the Panama City Inlet. On the good days we would hit these big bull redfish by bouncing jigs on the bottom, and it would be some great action. The reds were fifteen or twenty pounds, and they fought like crazy.

If the redfish weren't there we would be looking for alternative action. One of the fish that brought us great enjoyment on the slow days were big topsail catfish. These fish were three to five pounds, and they would readily bite our artificials. We figured out how to use a de-hooker to get them off the lines. We'd bring them up to the boat, grab the leader with the left hand and the de-hooker in the right hand, and by pulling up on the de-hooker and down on the leader the catfish would fall off the line. But in the meantime the catfish would be swinging in the breeze throwing slime in every direction. The leader and lure would be covered with slime. We could actually sometimes aim the slime at someone else on the boat. There were many a time when Gary or somebody would take the brunt of the abuse.

I remember one time; it was so funny. On top of everything else Terry, who at the time was probably six years old, was just on fire with getting these catfish to biting his lure. And Gary couldn't get a bite to save himself. So here was my six year old, starting out giving Gary advice on how to work his lure, and how fast to work it. He was hooking catfish and offering the rod to Gary to see if Gary wanted to wind them up.

That was a funny time. I can still see Terry asking, "Hey, Mr. Leff, would you like to take my rod? I've got one." Gary was a great guy. I sure miss him and his boys and the great times we had either in Miami Beach or Panama City, Florida.

The Captain Jumped

I really shook up Don Deitrich one time on a dolphin and swordfish trip. Don and his guest liked to fly fish for dolphin or catch dolphin on bait, whatever was working at the time. We were running offshore, looking for floating debris, and we were lucky enough to find plenty. I ran right over a big chunk of wood. There were no fish there, and there was no apparent damage to the boat. After checking the area out thoroughly and seeing there were no fish, we headed on our way again.

I heard a clunking sound repeatedly. I stopped and trimmed the engines out of the water but there didn't appear to be a problem. I couldn't figure out what the noise was so I started running again, but the plunking and banging started again. So I stopped again.

The boat had a transom mounted transducer with a stainless bracket screwed to the back of the boat, and the transmitter/receiver for the depth finder was fastened to the bracket. In those days a lot of boats had their transducers mounted that way. At any rate, my transom mount transducer had apparently been broken off the boat when I hit the log and it was banging along. There was no telling what kind of damage would end up happening with it that way.

This was when I still had my Dusky 256 and didn't use a mate. There were just the three of us there, and Don and his guest were sitting up front while I ran the boat from the helm station. At any rate, I stopped the boat and they got up to see what was going on. I took off my pliers, and took out my wallet, took off my sunglasses, and emptied my pockets. I grabbed my pliers and stepped out on the dive platform and did a beautiful dive into the ocean. I swam under the boat and cut the cable to the transducer. Then I threw the transducer in the boat, threw my pliers in the boat, and climbed back in.

The guys were standing there with their mouths agape and their eyes wide open. I said, "Is everything OK?"

They said, "We didn't know why the captain was abandoning ship, but we were definitely in a state of shock."

You should tell your co-riders on the boat when you are planning on abandoning ship for no reason whatsoever.

Tournament Wins

Burning Marlin Tournament in Bimini

Over the years I've been pretty lucky in tournaments. One that just popped into my head was the Burning Marlin Tournament in Bimini. Rick Benitez chartered me for himself, his daughter, and six year old grandson, Victor. This was a good fun tournament sponsored by the Guy Harvey Resorts at Bimini Sands in South Bimini. The tournament had several categories: inshore, reef, and offshore.

From the time we got there we could do no wrong. We went to a sunken barge back up on the Bank and caught mangrove snappers, and barracudas, and grunts until we had filled several categories of species and maximum quantities. Then we moved to a ledge off the dropoff and caught almaco jacks, and cero mackerel, and more barracudas, and filled out several more categories. Then we trolled the edge and caught barracudas and yellow jacks and, interesting enough, we were in a new category and could catch the same types of fish all over again. When all was a said and done, Victor was the adult master angler for the whole tournament. We won the reef category and the offshore category. But we sort of blew it at the same time. We could have won the inshore category too because we had some locations we could have gone to and caught some bonefish, but I didn't think of it in time.

The committee came to us and asked us if we would forfeit the Junior Angler trophy since our junior angler, six-year-old Victor, had won the tournament Master Angler trophy. They recognized that we could have demanded that one too, but we agreed with them so they could give the Junior Angler trophy to a little girl. We said that would only be right, so we spread the wealth around a little bit. My young angler received a beautiful trophy and several other awards.

After the awards ceremony an artist made an excellent rebar impression of a blue marlin. They had stuffed this marlin with coconuts and coconut leaves and all kinds of combustible material. They lit it on fire out on the beach and made an amazing bonfire. After the combustibles had burned away the marlin shaped rebar was glowing beautifully in the dark. This is how the Burning Marlin Tournament got its name and I'm glad the tournament committee sent us photos of it. That was a really neat victory.

Pompano Rodeo

I had an interesting near-victory in the Pompano Rodeo where I was fishing on the *Red Head*. The owner was a gentleman in his late sixties named Lou Skulnick, and he had brought a young man to come with him. On the first day of the tournament we were going to fish for blue marlin and big dolphin, as I had success with that one other time in a previous tournament.

We had just gotten out and started trolling when the steering on the boat went out. So I worked my way back to Harbor Towne. Mr. Skulnick had called up on the phone as we were going down the Intracoastal and arranged for them to be standing by to fix our steering so we could get back to the tournament. Sure enough, we got back to the dock and tied up;

they fixed the steering, and we headed back out of Port Everglades and headed offshore. In three or four hundred feet of water there was a beautiful rip. I put a spread of trolling baits out and in short order we hooked a beautiful blue marlin. We caught that marlin and it was something like 267 pounds. I felt confident that we were going to be hard to beat in the tournament. We didn't catch anything else that day, but we did catch a big dolphin the following day.

And lo and behold, we were beaten out of first place in the tournament by a boat that caught two blue marlin. For many years there were no blue marlin caught in the Pompano Rodeo, but that year there were several. So our 267 blue and big dolphin were beaten by a guy who caught two blue marlin. Those doggone blue marlins in the Pompano Rodeo have been hard on me. We came in second that year.

There was another year with Lou Skulnick and his son that we had a successful blue marlin story. The same year we won second place in the Pompano Rodeo, we were in the Miami Billfish Tournament. Al Adams was my mate, and on the last day of the tournament we were fishing just north of Government Cut. We caught a couple of sailfish, and lo and behold, in the waning minutes of the tournament, we hooked a blue marlin. We wanted to catch this fish because blue marlin were three times as many tournament points as sailfish. But we were running out of time. We had to be at the dock by 5:30 or all the fish would be disqualified. Having caught and released that blue marlin we got back to the dock at 5:25. We came in the money in that tournament thanks to that blue marlin.

Another year we had two boats with the same name in the tournament. I had fished on the *Hip-Knee-Tized* for several years. It belonged to Dr. Steve Roy who was a medical inventor and owned an artificial knee and hip replacement company. We had some great tournaments together. There were two brothers, Mike and Mark Rudnick, who were salesmen for Steve's company who also fished with us. Also aboard were Ralph Renick from WTVJ, a cameraman, and me as their captain.

Mark Rudnick and I and Ralph Renick would leave from Haulover and catch pilchards. We would then run up the beach and pick up Mike Rudkin and Steve Roy. We would always do well in the tournament, big tunas and blackfin tunas and stuff. Our team had grown because the children wanted to fish now, so we now had the *Hip-Knee-Tized II*. Now Mark and Ralph and I would leave out of Haulover and catch enough bait for two boats. We'd give the other boat bait and rig up wire leaders and so forth. We'd both go off the Steeple and anchor up. We'd chum with live pilchards and fish for blackfin tunas and kingfish, and occasionally a cobia or a sailfish. We were a team that was hard to beat.

We were the first team to anchor in the Pompano Rodeo and we really tore it up. It looked like we were going to win the tournament and the *Hip-Knee-Tize II* was going to come in the money. But I'll be doggone if on the last day another boat didn't catch a 500 pound blue marlin and knocked us down to second place. Our boats took second place and fourth place.

At the awards we had a big table with all our anglers and the rest of our team. The tournament officials were going crazy announcing that, "Second place went to *Hip-Knee-Tize;* and fourth place went to *Hip-Knee-Tized II?*" "First place blackfin tuna *Hip-Knee-Tize*, second place *Hip-Knee-Tize II* ?" It went down the list that way.

It was really a lot of fun with the Steve Roy fishing team on the the *Hip-Knee-Tize* and the *Hip-Knee-Tize II* with Mark and

Mike Rudkin, and Ralph Renick, and Ralph Renick Jr. We have a long list of great things we've done together. Ralph has always been a great asset in my life and I cannot thank him enough for all the great things he has done for me over the years.

Miami Billfish Tournament

It was interesting, I caught three blue marlin in three years and all three were caught in tournaments. I chartered everyday and never caught one except in tournaments. Another blue marlin pretty close to the same time gave us another victory in the Miami Billfish Tournament.

I was fishing with Bill MacDonald and his band of cohorts on his thirty-foot Scarab Sport. We were kite fishing with live mullet. It was the first year the Miami Billfish Tournament was a release tournament. The rule is that if the leader reaches the rod tip, or anybody on the boat touches the leader, the fish is considered caught. We were fishing off Key Biscayne and every time Bill went to relieve himself a sailfish would pop up on the kite. I think we caught three sailfish that day if I'm not mistaken. It was my turn to go relieve myself and Bill said, "Oh, there's a sailfish on the kite." I zipped myself up and as I turned here was this 300 pound blue marlin, head and shoulders out of the water eating the mullet.

I said, "Bill, that the biggest sailfish I've ever seen."

Bill asked, "Well, what do I, what do I do?" He had twenty-pound test with a fifty-pound leader, a Penn International, and a seven-foot medium action rod. This was no tackle for a 300 pound blue marlin.

I said, "Just wind down tight and set the hook and hope for the best." He wound tight and set the hook and held on tight. The marlin started swimming slowly to the north. The stern of the boat was headed north so I backed down going along with the fish. I said, "Bill, this fish doesn't even know he's hooked. He's just swimming along to the north. You're going to have to put some pressure on him. Set the hook really hard and let him know he's in trouble. If he comes up and jumps we might be able to get the leader and get a release."

So Bill wound down on him and put his thumb on the spool, gave it three or four sharp jabs, and thankfully nothing broke. We could see the blue marlin down there shaking his head, so I started throttling down on the engines in reverse. The fish started coming to the surface, so I gave it full speed reverse. The engines made a high winding noise and died. There was something about those Mercury engines that if you punched them in reverse they would throttle up and then die completely. So now I couldn't get the engines started and we were drifting backwards. And here came the blue marlin, straight up in the air. I don't know what Bill did to it when he set the hook, but the fish went straight up in the air three quarters of his length out of the water. It fell over on his back, belly up with his bill pointed right straight at the transom. As the boat glided backwards, and the marlin glided forward, the fish went right between the motors and crashed into the transom. So now Bill had the leader wound all the way on to the reel. The fish hit the transom and rolled over and sank under the engines.

Bill cleared the engines and the marlin took off running and jumping. We had a legitimate catch and release, so I called the committee boat and told them we had caught and released a blue marlin, but we were still holding onto it waiting for him to chew through the leader so we could let him go without a bunch of line hanging from his mouth. We caught that fish, but it was nip and tuck. The last day we did not catch a fish.

The previous year there was a prize of $25,000 or $50,000 to whoever caught a blue, a white, and a sail. This year, being the first year it was a release tournament, there was no more big prize for that. But we had several sailfish, and we had the blue marlin, and on the last day we had a white marlin chase a goggle eye into a weed patch, or we may have caught a white marlin too.

Mike Leach, the then president of the IGFA, almost caught us on points in the tournament because on the last day he caught a couple of white marlin, and with the point schedule the way it was, we only ended up beating him by one fish. So it was a close race right up until the end. But we ended up winning that tournament, and what a great time it was, and what a great friend Bill MacDonald was.

Anyone who knows me knows that I am averse to bananas on the boat, not just a little, more like passionately. In my first book I told about the Fruit of the Loom gentleman and me, and our discussion about bananas and how that was the end of bananas in the Fruit of the Loom advertising. That took place because Don was the customer who brought Jack from Fruit of the Loom on the boat.

Don and Sandy fished with me the third Wednesday of every month. In the spring following the Fruit of the Loom incident Don and Sandy decided they wanted to fish the Miami Billfish Tournament. That was back in the 90s when I fished by myself without a mate. We agreed that Don and his son-in-law and Sandy would fish on the boat. The tournament was run out of Miami Beach Marina so I would run my boat down to Government Cut, and my sister would get on the boat, and she and I would go out and catch herring. Then we would come back at 7:30 and pick up Don and Sandy and the son-in-law and we would go out and fish the tournament.

The first day Sue and I went out to catch the herring but they were a little late to bite, so we got back to the dock about five minutes late. The tournament started at eight so we expected our party to be on the dock; but they weren't there. I started looking all over for them. We didn't have cell phones yet, so I was looking all over for them but didn't see them. Somebody said they had been there earlier but didn't know where they went. By ten minutes to eight I still couldn't find them and I started to worry.

Then at five minutes till eight they came running down the dock and jumped on the boat. And we took off to the starting line. It was a Bimini start and we were just pulling into the jetties when the starter said go. We were a little behind the fleet when we started chugging out to the southeast. It was beautiful flat calm water with a light west wind. Just outside of the Cuban Hole there was just a faint rip. I ran right over it and then circled back around. When I got back to the rip I fired out the first herring on a spinning rod and let it run out. As I was baiting the second hook, and before I got it in the water, we got a strike on the first bait. Sandy picked it up and he had a sailfish on. We caught the sailfish and released it. It was the first sailfish of the tournament and it put us in first place.

I swung back into that rip and got two baits out and we hooked two fish. Don took the first fish and Sandy took the second one. Don caught a bonito and Sandy caught a sailfish. Now we had the first two sailfish of the tournament. When the dust settled after fishing for two and a half days, we caught six sailfish the first day, five the second day, and one on the third day. Sandy caught the vast majority of the fish.

We went through all kinds of missteps, like missing the Bimini start the first day, and our tackle box fell over and spilled all our hooks. Don was on the floor cleaning those up while Sandy caught the first sailfish.

On the second day Sandy was fighting a sailfish and the nut that holds down the rotator head on the spinning reel came loose, and the rotating head started binding up on the spool. I sat next to Sandy and went through the motions while he opened the bail, took off the spool and put it in a drink holder, tightened up the rotator nut, put the spool back on, put the drive nut back on, closed the bail and caught a sailfish - completely unassisted and within the rules of the tournament.

We caught six sailfish the first day, five the second day, and one the third day and were in first place for the entire tournament. And what a thrill it was to win.

So, let's go back to the first day. How come those guys didn't get to the boat until five minutes till eight? Don said, "Well, you know, we got down to the dock and it wasn't even seven o'clock yet, more like six thirty. They rushed me so much I didn't get a chance to take my morning constitutional, so I went in the men's room and dropped my drawers. I sat down there and I saw that I was wearing Fruit of the Loom underwear. So I did my thing, and I got straightened up, and I ran out of there and told the guys we gotta go back and change my underwear."

So, they drove from Miami Beach Marina, all the way back up to Aventura, and went up to the top floor of a highrise building. Don changed into his red silk underwear; they got back in the car, got caught in rush hour traffic, and got to the boat at five minutes to eight. It was a good thing. Because of that Don wore his red silk underwear the whole tournament and, lo and behold, we won because he changed out of those Fruit of the Looms with the bananas on them.

It was a great event. We had a lot of fun and we went on to fish some other tournaments and did really well in those too. Don and Sandy were a blessing to fish with and I loved every minute we spent together.

I think a little history of the Miami Billfish Tournament is in order. That was a tournament that went on every year for thirty years. When it became the first release tournament, Ft. Lauderdale and West Palm Beach soon followed. In time the tournament began to lose participants and was in danger of collapsing. In response to this lack of outside interest it was converted to a fun fish tournament. But owners, captains, and anglers liked the prize money and Calcuttas of the older tournaments and stopped registering. On account of this the tournament went into hibernation in hopes of coming up with some idea to reinvigorate it.

I won that last Miami Billfish Tournament. In that tournament I fished it with David Barkus, a long time customer going all the way back to when he was a kid, and a new customer who was a friend of his. We won that tournament because of an advantage we had through years of experience.

The first day we fished off Key Biscayne. We fished off Government Cut and Miami Beach the second day. The wind blew about fifteen miles an hour and everybody was kite fishing. We hooked multiple sailfish first thing in the morning of the first day and we caught them all. But unfortunately the mate had the rod in his hand when one sailfish ate the bait and we had to disqualify that one. The bottom line is we caught a lot of sailfish the first day.

But on the second day the wind quit. Now everyone was kite fishing with helium balloons. To keep the balloons up and out behind their boats they had to keep driving south against the wind. So all these boats were driving south against the wind and nobody was catching much. There was a good strong north current, so I told Abie, my mate, to forget about the kite. Let's fish the flat lines and drift with the current. If the kite will fly, fine, but if not we'll just fish the flat lines. So here we were at the Miami Sea Buoy and there were all these boats driving to the south, keeping their kites up and fighting the current. As we drifted through the fleet we caught a couple of sailfish. Then we ran back south and drifted through the fleet again and caught a couple more. This happened several times and we just kept picking away at the sailfish. The big difference was that everyone else was driving against the current, and we were drifting with the current. In the nature of things in the Gulf Stream, big predator fish swim against the current expecting the baitfish to drift north at the speed of the current. A proper presentation of your bait is to be drifting at about the speed of the current. I had learned this when I lost a tournament many years before when it was blowing thirty out of the north and all the big boats were driving north into the wind and with the current, catching fish like crazy. I was drifting with the wind that was opposing the current and we were not even seeing any fish. Late in the afternoon I figured everyone else was drifting north and catching fish, so I've got to try it, and sure enough we finally saw a couple of fish. I learned from that to go with the current and it paid off in the very last Miami Billfish Tournament.

Two Beers

So, I'm seventy-one years old. Want to make a guess how many beers I've drunk in my life? I'll save you a lot of frustration. I've had two beers. They were both Michelobs, and they were both the same afternoon.

Joe Labonte had come down from Boston, MA, to work as my mate for the winter as he had for several years. Joe was a heavy equipment operator up north and worked for me in the wintertime on the charter boat *Top Luck* out of the Castaways Hotel. Here we were, it was the middle of September and it was hotter than all get out. The humidity was through the ceiling. We were offshore on a charter with an all day trip and the dolphin were snapping. I mean all the little dolphin you could ever ask for, hundreds of them.

It was so hot and humid that I'd run the boat for a while and then go down in the cockpit. Then Joe would come up and run the boat. And then we would switch places because up on the bridge we had a little breeze to cool off, and we could have a chance to sit down. In the cockpit it was hot and humid and we had to run around in circles.

This went on for hours, but we had a box full of dolphin. I was up on the bridge and called down, "Hey Joe, throw me some water."

"We're out of water."

"Well, let me have a coke."

"We're out of cokes."

"Well, what do you have to drink down there?"

He said, "Bouncer, all we've got is Michelob."

I said, "No. I'm not even twenty-one yet. I don't drink. Thank you anyway. I sure wish we had something to drink."

We went on about our way fishing. We were trolling down off of Key Biscayne about ten or twelve miles offshore, and the fishing had slowed down a little bit. A little while later I called back down, "Joe, are you sure there's no water?" I hesitated. "No sodas? I gotta have something. Give me one of those beers."

So I drank a Michelob. To me it didn't taste very good, but it did quench my thirst a little bit. And I ran the boat for a little while longer. It was still slow fishing. Joe was sitting at the top of the ladder and I was running the boat. We didn't trade off anymore because things had slowed down a lot. We went on for a while and I was just dying of thirst. I think the first beer made me thirstier. I said, "Joe, I gotta have something to drink. I guess I'll have to have another beer."

So he gave me another Michelob and I drank it. And now I'm feeling it. Oh my gosh! What is this feeling? Now bear in mind, I had never had alcohol before in my life. I was dehydrated and I had drunk two beers. I got really goofy, and then it was time to go home. I was trying to run back to Haulover Inlet, but I was totally wasted. I couldn't find the inlet. I couldn't figure what in the world I was doing. Joe had to take the wheel. He ran the boat for a while and put it in the slip. I stumbled down off the bridge. When we got back we put the fish on the dock and I got squared away a bit.

Those were my first beer ever, my second beer ever, and my last beer ever. That's the rare story of a fishing captain who has only drunk two beers in his whole life. But they sure did the job of getting me a little bit tipsy there.

Great White Shark

I was fishing in the Pompano Rodeo with Jim Atria on his boat the *Jennifer Lyn* in the early 1980s. We had fished three tournaments in a row, the Miami Billfish Tournament, the Ft. Lauderdale Billfish Tournament, and now the Pompano Rodeo, altogether on the same boat. The mates had changed, but for this tournament my mate was Jack Plachter, a famous captain of long time standing over the years running different kinds of private boats and charter boats as well.

We were targeting blue marlin. We had caught a big white and numerous dolphins and were currently in second place, thirty-nine pounds behind the *Webb Tide* with Jerry Webb, and Terry Guthrie, and Mike Marino. We had shared equipment and baits for all three tournaments. So here we were in the last tournament. They were in first place by thirty-nine pounds, and we were in second place. We were twenty miles offshore trolling to the east and I spotted a small oil slick up ahead. This is frequently indicative of fish feeding where they will tear a fish apart and the oils will rise to the surface. We were aimed straight into the sun. I told Jack there was a slick up ahead and then I saw something that looked like it was floating in the slick. I said, "I think we have a swordfish kill."

Jack jumped into action making a shark rig because every once in a while we'd come across a swordfish that had just been killed by a big mako shark. It would be a great thrill to catch the mako, even though it would not be eligible for the tournament. As I approached, all I could see was something sticking up in the oil slick. Jack told Jim Atria to grab the flying gaff and stand at the port side of the cockpit and gaff anything that floated by. In the meantime the sun was in my eyes and I had no good vision of how big the object was. I lined it up to come down the port side, and as I did Jim hollered, "I need help here."

I turned around and he had the flying gaff stuck in this huge swordfish. Jack came over to help him and I came down from the bridge. We opened the tuna door and pulled the swordfish into the boat. It was still quivering. The tail was completely chopped off and the bill was chopped off right across the face. I went back up onto the bridge to see if I could see the shark. Jack cut a chunk of meat off the swordfish tail and put it on a shark rig and threw it out. Before long here came this behemoth, a great white shark probably twelve or fourteen hundred pounds. It would glide around the boat effortlessly, and it was so big we couldn't even see its tail move. It seemed to be eyeballing us and following us as if to ask what we had done with its breakfast.

This white shark wasn't going to be fooled easily. We tried everything with this nice strip of swordfish meat, but he just wouldn't bite. Finally after quite a while of gawking at this shark I told Jack to gut the swordfish; throw some guts in the water and put the heart on one of our two hooks along with the chunk of meat. Jack did as I suggested, threw some guts in the water, and the great white ate them. He threw in the swordfish chunk along with its heart out the back of the boat.

In short order the shark ate the bait. So the shark was swimming along behind the boat looking right at us. But I knew if we hooked it, it was going to be a tough shot.

I said, "Just let him eat the bait and wait until he turns another angle." As he turned around to head straight away from us I told Jim to engage the Penn Eighty International. It was full of brand new eighty-pound test with number fifteen wire. As the shark turned away from us I gunned the boat and Jim leaned back repeatedly trying to set the hook. After I ran off 200 feet of line I stopped the boat. And there was the shark on the surface swimming right back toward the boat. I told Jim to try to set the hook again. I gunned the motor and Jim hauled on the line, but the shark just kept following the boat. We tried it again, and somehow the shark just let go of everything. The hooks and the wire and everything came out of his mouth.

We wound it in and here was the leader wire almost as heavy as coat hanger wire. Thirty-nine inches from the hook, the wire was bent 180 degrees. The wire went straight up, made a U-turn and went straight down. That was where the wire had been wrapped around the corner of the shark's jaw. From the bend in the wire to the hook was more than three feet and that told us how deep inside his mouth those hooks were.

I'll be a son of a gun if I didn't overthink things. I waited until he was pointed straight away to hook him and in so doing it bent the wire around his jaw. There was no way there was any pressure put on the hook, and all he did was to turn around and come back looking at us.

Now the shark was behind the boat again and we spent an hour trying to catch it. Finally I hollered down from the bridge, "It's up to you guys. We're only thirty-nine pounds out of first place in this tournament, or we can fish for this shark." The decision was made to go try to win the tournament. It wasn't ten minutes later we caught a big wahoo. The *Webb Tide* called and wanted to know how big our wahoo was. I told them that they should be sweating because if they didn't catch something it was going to be really close.

Fishing ended at one o'clock, and again Terry Guthrie on the *Webb Tide* called and asked, "So, how big is your wahoo?"

I said, "Oh, it's sixty or seventy pounds." I was joking with him. I knew it wasn't that big.

Terry said, "You guys win. We'll see you at the awards tonight." Then they shut down their radio and took off running back to the dock. I kept trying to call them on the radio to tell them I was joking.

The *Webb Tide* and the *Jennifer Lyn* were told at the end of fishing that we had to report to the headquarters because the press wanted to talk to us at the end of the tournament. Apparently we were first and second in the tournament one way or another. As we were pulling up to the dock the *Webb Tide* was leaving. I was hollering, "Don't go, don't go!" They said they would get a table for us together tonight and left.

So we pulled in with our white marlin, dolphin, and wahoo, and we needed thirty-nine pounds to tie, or forty pounds to win the tournament. Even thirty-nine and a half would win the tournament. Our wahoo weighed thirty-eight and a half pounds. We took second place by a half-pound.

The awards dinner was quite an event for us. At our table were the crews from *Jennifer Lynn*, *Webb Tide,* and *Quetzal*. *Webb Tide* had come in first; we were second, and *Quetzal*, with Eddie and Jenny Wheeler, won the ladies division. Our table was covered over in tournament trophies from the many categories we won collectively.

As a sidebar, when we got back to the dock we called Port O Call Seafood to see if they wanted to buy our swordfish. They said, "Yeah, we'll buy your swordfish, and here's our pricelist. If the swordfish is whole and it is cored out, we pay three dollars a pound. If the swordfish is shark bit then we pay one dollar a pound." They don't want to buy shark bit swordfish because they may have been floating on the surface for hours in hot water and started to spoil. Well we knew that ours had not been floating in the water and had not degenerated. We had packed it in ice when we pulled it into the boat still quivering. So we cored it out and cut the head and fins off. All the guts were gone and we cut the body off forward of the anal fin where there were no more teeth marks. So we had the biggest part of the body of the swordfish. We kept parts of the tail section to take home and eat ourselves, and we had this big old chunk of swordfish to take to the Port O Call. All we had left was just a big barrel shaped piece of swordfish meat, but it still weighed 300 pounds. That swordfish in whole condition was probably 500 pounds or better. What a story to tell, big white marlin, big dolphin, a great white shark to remember, and high places in the tournament – really great memories.

Momma Cat

When I kept my boat at Keystone Point Marina in North Miami, there was a cat I called Momma Cat that came by to greet me every morning. As soon as I drove my truck into the marina to park, Momma Cat would come running from wherever she was to meet me at my truck door. She would escort me back and forth every trip I made to my boat to unload my fishing gear and so forth. When I would get on the boat and start setting up for the day she would jump on the boat and sit on the helm seat right by the steering wheel while I was rigging rods or whatever I was doing. Then when I was ready to go fishing she would jump off the boat and I would take off with my charter. As I was backing into my slip when I returned in the afternoon, she would come running from wherever she was hiding, and she would be quivering on the corner of the dock as I backed in. She would immediately jump onto my captain's seat and put her head under my hand so I could scratch her ears. It was such a heartwarming relationship, me and Momma Cat.

One day I was down just puttering around on the boat, and I was tied up with my starboard side to the floating dock. Momma Cat was hanging out with me on the boat. Her son, Morris, was also on the boat hanging out. I needed to fuel up, so I untied the boat and pushed from the starboard side of the boat over to the fuel dock which made me port side to the dock. I tied the boat up and was fueling it and something made a noise. Morris jumped off the boat to investigate. He thought we were starboard side to the dock, but he didn't realize that when I moved the boat we were port side to. As he jumped, he screamed in midair as he realized he was suspended over the water. He splashed down and took off swimming for dry land.

Momma Cat heard him scream and jumped over to investigate. Once again, she remembered us being tied up starboard side to the dock, but she also hadn't realized the boat had moved. So Momma Cat ended up in the water too. I grabbed Momma Cat and lifted her in the boat. Morris, in his infinite wisdom, had swum to the end of the dock where I had been tied up. There was an access hole in the end of the floating dock and he crawled in. So now he was inside the dock yowling his head off. My sister, Sue, had to climb down in the water and get around to the seawall end of the dock to coax Morris out. She got a hold of him and placed him up on the dock, and then climbed up on the dock herself.

It wasn't enough chaos that Momma Cat and Morris had both fallen in the water. After this fiasco was over I was walking over to the men's room. That was a 200 foot walk from where I had fueled up the boat, and when I was walking down the dock Baby Cat, Momma Cat's baby from a new litter, was walking with me like a dog on a leash right next to the water. That dumb little cat walked right off the dock into the water on the same day the other two cats jumped overboard. It was the craziest thing I ever saw.

Momma Cat went on to have quite a history. I did TV fishing reports with Ralph Renick, Jr. They would come to the dock on Friday morning and videotape my fishing report and fishing tips. Many times, with Momma Cat there, she would be part of the show.

One day we were rigging ballyhoo and Ralph went to put his camera in the car. While I was cleaning up the table a pelican landed on the dock. When Momma Cat would turn away the pelican would try to sneak up and steal a ballyhoo. But Momma Cat would sense the pelican and turn around and hiss at it. The pelican would back off and this would go on over and over again, the pelican trying to sneak up and steal the ballyhoos while Momma Cat would protect the ballyhoo. They did this so long that Ralph Renick got his camera back out and videotaped the show with the pelican and Momma Cat sparring over the ballyhoo. The video went worldwide.

Then there was one other great cat story. Momma Cat loved to hang out with me. I mean she was with me constantly when I was at the dock. One day I was puttering around and I had to go over to Haulover Docks to check the bait in my bait pen. I didn't notice where Momma Cat was and I untied the boat and headed over to Haulover Docks. Moving down along the dock Momma Cat was very apprehensive. 'What's this? The boat's moving?' She looked over the side and there was water on both sides. She looked so nervous. And then I hit the open bay and opened up the throttle. You would have thought that I was a police boat or a fireboat because I had the loudest animated siren, screaming her head off as I ran across the bay. I got over and checked my bait cage, and going back at full speed here goes the siren again. She got off the boat in a hurry when we got back to the dock.

But I loved Momma Cat. She had such a personality and I always have fond memories of her.

Ron Jon's Crab

Ron Jon Cook was a great mate of mine. This time Ron Jon and I had a two-boat trip to Bimini. We were joined by Matt Tambor in one boat, and Ron Jon and I were on another boat. It was a two-boat group of guys from Wisconsin. We were in my charter boat, Bouncer's Dusky 33, and Matty was borrowing a Contender from one of his friends, and the friend came along as the mate. We were staying at the Big Game Club.

We had cast nets and everything you could possibly need, but the other boat was little short on supplies. Particularly, they did not have a cast net. On the first day we went up on the bank and anchored up on a wreck. While we were there the ballyhoo came up, so we threw the cast net so we would have live ballyhoo in case we needed them during the trip. Then we met up with the other boat about two o'clock in the afternoon and they said they needed some ballyhoo. So Ron Jon gave them a couple of dozen, and as we drifted apart Matt Tambor said, "Hey I need more ballyhoo than that." So Ron Jon grabbed another six ballyhoo and threw them at Matt and hit him.

As soon as he did it he said, "Oh, I should not have done that. I will pay for that later on."

I didn't know all the goings on about Matty yet. We were pretty good friends, and later we became great friends. But Ron Jon and Matt were long time good buddies. The bottom line was that Ron Jon was worried about Matt getting even for being hit with the ballyhoo.

We fished out the day and I don't remember any of the particulars about what we caught. These guys were pretty good fishermen and typically in Bimini it was amberjacks, and yellowtails, and sharks, and groupers, and kingfish, and mackerel, just a really lot of fun.

The next day we decided we would go for pilchards in the canals on the south island. So Ron Jon and I went up a couple of canals and found a huge school of pilchards. Ron threw the net a few times and we filled the live well. These were sandy key pilchards and they die really easy. We loaned our cast net to Matty because it made more sense for him to catch his own pilchards. We didn't want to catch them and put them in our live well, and then net them and put them in his live well. That would have beaten them up a lot. It would be better for Matt to catch them and dump them right in his own live well. We gave Matty our cast net and told him where to go, then we went out on our own way fishing.

I remember we had really great fishing. I don't remember the details, but I remember it was good. When we got in to the dock I was cleaning fish and Ron Jon was on the boat with me making a conch salad. He was chopping all his vegetables and conch and mixing up his salad for the six guys on the charter as well as the crewmembers on the two boats. While we were cleaning and prepping, Matty came by to shoot the breeze for a few minutes and then left. Shortly after he left he came back to shoot the breeze again. Ron finished making his conch salad, and I cleaned the fish and then the boat. After that we went and got cleaned up for dinner. We went to the Big Game Club restaurant and had our fish cooked up and had a great dinner. All the guys from the boats wanted to go bar hopping, and I went back to the room to chill. I was resting in the room and finally fell asleep. Ron Jon woke me up coming in the room. He went in the bathroom, and came back out. He crawled under the covers and screamed, "That doggone maid." And he threw something across the room.

I said, "What happened?"

He said, "That dumb maid left a damp towel in my bedding. Now my bed's all damp. Doggone it!"

So, the lights were out and I rolled over to go to sleep while Ron Jon settled down. It was maybe three or four minutes and the expletives came screaming out of Ron Jon again and I rolled over. He was dancing on top of his bed. There was all kinds of hollering and swearing, cuss words and everything else, and he looked like some kind of crazy hieroglyphic dancer dancing on top of his bed. He jumped off the bed finally and turned on the light. "That damn Matt Tambour. Look what he's done."

By now this giant blue claw crab was on the floor and Ron Jon scooped it into the wastebasket. This crab had to be ten or twelve inches across the shell, plus the claws. It was madder than a hornet, and Ron Jon was a total wreck. Somehow this blue crab has gotten into Ron Jon's bed. He said, "I'm going to take this thing out and dump it in the bushes."

I said, "Oh, no. He won't survive. You've got to go dump it in the water." So he dumped the crab in the water and went upstairs and pounded on Matty's door. But Matty would not answer the door, so Ron Jon came back downstairs and climbed into bed, muttering and groaning, and cussing Matty like there's no tomorrow.

The next day Matty shared his side of the story. He had found one of the maids and gotten a key to our room. He had caught this blue crab in the cast net while he was catching pilchards in the morning. They pestered the crab with a bridle needle all day just to keep it mad and irritated. They pestered the devil out of it, and then he put it in Ron Jon's bed and put the damp towel on top of it, and made up the bed. He made it back down to our boat, and when he was down there shooting the breeze with us, he asked which bed I was sleeping in. We had told him I was sleeping closest to the sliding glass door, which I was.

In the morning when we started discussing the crab story I started chewing him out and told him I was sleeping closest to the bathroom and I got the crab, just to have a little fun with him. But what a crazy event that was. That was the blue claw crab event in Bimini, never to be forgotten.

Seasick

Here's a question I hear all the time, "Hey, Bouncer, you ever been seasick?" Well, I've been close, but I've never been seasick. My first exposure to seasickness was when I was probably eight years old. Jack Lentz owned a twenty-one foot Chris Craft kit boat. It was a brown and white cabin boat that and had a small, six-cylinder gas engine. He kept it in Keystone Point. He was gracious enough to invite my dad and me to fish with him on a number of occasions.

This time Jack brought his daughter, Jill. So we got out there fishing and Jill was eating vanilla wafers. It wasn't long before she got seasick. Well, it was disgusting. Here was all this beautiful blond hair hanging in front of her face as she vomited half digested vanilla wafers overboard. After all this time, which is now what, over sixty-two years, I have never eaten a vanilla wafer – I just can't get past that picture. But that was my first exposure to seasickness.

My next real concern with seasickness, I was probably about fifteen years old. On weekends I worked on all day trips along with Billy Strudwick, with Captain Dick on the *Silverfin* out of 163rd Street. On this one trip all of a sudden I began feeling really sick. I was headachy, feverish, and throwing up overboard on the downwind side of the boat. No! Not after all these years and all these future plans; I can't be seasick. I love

70

the ocean. I go on the ocean every chance I get. I've never been seasick, and it wasn't even extra rough. I was thinking that I was going to be a captain and fish all my life – I couldn't get seasick. What am I going to do? Oh my God, and now I feel feverish and I've got chills, and I'm puking.

I got home and I didn't get any better. I woke up in the morning and was still just as sick, still throwing up and still feverish. Oh my God, I'm so glad that I have the flu. I was scared to death that I was seasick, but lo and behold, it was just a common, rotten, miserable flu. I can still be a sea captain, and a flats guide, and a fisherman. All my dreams are saved. Thank you goodness, flu. That was a really life threatening event there. To have been seasick would have been the end of the world.

So the next time I have to admit to dealing with seasickness we were in the Tongue of the Ocean between Chubb Cay and Andros. It was blowing pretty good. The seas were four to six feet and we were trolling for blue marlin on a fifty-five or sixty foot Hatteras. We had been trolling all day and it was getting kind of mid afternoon. It's a pretty good haul from Andros back to Chubb, so we started trolling in that direction. Lo and behold, the port engine died. Seconds later the starboard engine died. The captain was in a tight circle. "What's happened?"

Oh, we were out of fuel. The captain forgot to change fuel tanks in the morning. All he had to do was throw a valve. But now the captain wasn't sure how to prime the engines to start them again. He was a really nice and really knowledgeable captain, but we were kind of stuck. Fortunately, having worked on charter boats and having rebuilt diesel engines and primed fuel systems and so forth, I told him to relax. I would take care of it. I climbed down into this 160 or 170 degree engine room, with the boat laying in the trough and rolling back and forth. I had to crack the return lines on the generator and fill a bucket with diesel fuel. And now I've got the diesel fumes from that in my face. I have to take the primary filters off the big engines and fill them with fuel and screw them back on. Now I've got diesel fuel on my hands and all over me, and again it's hot as blazes, and the boat is rocking back and forth. Yeah, I can't deny it; I was getting a little queasy. Maybe a lot queasy. I was trying to decide whether to puke in the diesel fuel, or puke in the bilge, or try to get another bucket down there before this seasickness goes full bore.

The good news is, I got the engines primed and they fired right up. I got back out in the fresh air and we were on our way home. The queasiness may have had me down a little bit, but I didn't have to chum up any fish. I didn't have to puke, and all's well that ends well.

Unfortunately that has started an issue that has arisen two more times. One of my favorite places to fish in the entire world is on the *Timely Sale* owned by Marty Arostegui, and fished by him, Roberta, Martini, Daniela, and occasionally Allie. On that boat they have diesel inboards. On two occasions catching bait at Bug Light I was right next to the exhaust from the generator. The diesel fumes had me just tweaked enough that I moved to the other side of the boat.

But in all my years on the ocean with fifty-three years full time, and a good ten years prior to that growing up, those were the only seasickness, or near seasickness episodes I have ever had. Believe me when I tell you, I've seen a lot of seasick people, and I always feel sorry for them. But thank goodness, my episodes have been non-existent or very minor.

Tiny

James Robert Edwards, my good buddy Tiny, was mating for me when we both ran out of the Castaways. This day Tiny was working the cockpit and I was running the boat. It was late in the day and fishing had been tough, but we finally hit into a bunch of bonitos. Back then we'd have a lot of baits rigged in the bait box on fifteen foot piano wire leaders. Tiny was completely wiped out of baits in the water so I ran down to help him. I grabbed a trolling bait out of the bait box and flopped it out of the boat. We were good enough that we could flip a bait, a fifteen-foot leader would uncoil, and we'd snap it on the rod and put it out. I grabbed a bait and flipped it out and put it on the snap swivel. A bonito snatched the bait right out of my hand, hook, wire, and all. I grabbed another bait and flipped it out and a bonito snatched that one out of my hand. Tiny was a big guy with a really short fuse. He chewed me out and ran me back up onto the bridge and told me to leave his cockpit alone because that was his department.

Another day Tiny rode along with Phil Conklin and me as we were going to do some commercial bottom fishing on a forty-eight foot charter boat out of the Castaways. Chartering was really slow and we needed to make some money so we ran down off Government Cut where we often caught snowy groupers and Warsaw groupers. It was a rocky bottom in 300 feet of water. When we got there Tiny and Phil dropped baits down while I held the boat in position. Tiny was fishing with this nine-O with 100-pound monofilament on a pretty long solid fiberglass rod. Soon he got a really good fish on and started to fight it. He was not able to use a fighting belt because they didn't make one big enough to go around him, so he was losing this battle. Phil had some kind of cheap looking fighting belt clipped on, so he took the rod from Tiny. He was fighting this great fish when suddenly the pin broke out of the bottom of the belt and the butt end of the rod slid down until the reel was down against the top of the fighting belt. It was now a very difficult fight. Then the fish took off running. The belt was tight around Phil's waist, and the rod was down around his knees. Then the fish leveraged Phil right off the deck by his family jewels. He was screaming and hollering while he tried to back the drag off to get the pressure off. He finally got free from the belt and they put the rod in the rod holder, but lo and behold, they wound up big Warsaw grouper.

I remember another time I fished with Tiny on one of the big charter boats and it was pouring down rain. I was up on the bridge under the canvas top staying bone dry, and the customers were running out in raincoats to catch fish. But Tiny had to stay out there and work in the rain all day, one rainstorm after another. The only good thing was we had pretty good fishing. We caught three or four sailfish and a quite few big dolphin and a few bonitos, but poor Tiny sure got drenched that day. That was the way it was with Tiny.

Another time in 1966 we were working on the *Seabreeze* out of Pier Five in downtown Miami. We were very much into fishing artificial lures on our days off. We would fish on the downwind side of the boat while the customers would fish on the upwind side with natural baits. We either fished deep jigs, two or three ounces like bucktail with Mylar in them, or we used one-ounce Mylar jigs and let them sink. We would jig them up really fast predominantly targeting kingfish. We also occasionally threw popping plugs for blackfin tuna and dolphin.

But this story is about these ounce and a quarter white nylon jigs that had an outside layer of Mylar like tinsel off a Christmas tree. They were wrapped with blue thread and locally made. I would go in and buy two dozen at a time because that was my bread and butter for catching fish on the head boat. Tiny would go in and buy two dozen at a time too because he fished right next to me. As a matter of fact, one day I used one of those jigs and caught twenty-seven kingfish on a half day trip. By the time we were done fishing it was a bent up crinkly wire leader and a hook, and connecting the wire leader to the hook was a chewed up, hammered, bright shiny lead. And that's all I needed to catch the kingfish.

The story goes that we bought all these jigs at Commercial Fishing Supply in downtown Miami, and I bought so many on a regular basis that Dude Perkins, the operator of the store, put a label on the tray where those jigs were and called them Bouncer lures. Tiny went in there to buy jigs and he saw that label and never bought another one of those jigs. He would use a yellow jig, or an all white jig, or a red and white jig, but he would not use those with the Mylar strips on the outside because they were Bouncer lures, and that just made him mad at the proprietor of the tackle shop.

God bless these two friends who fish in a better place today, Dude Perkins and James Robert Edwards, better known as Tiny.

Abie's Secret Spots

I fished out of Haulover Inlet from 1956 until we moved down to Miami Beach Marina in 1997, so I was very familiar with all of the fishing spots out of Haulover for a long time. Now, having fished out of Government Cut for over twenty years, Abie Raymond and I decided to work our way north one Saturday to try and catch some bottom fish. I knew several spots between Government Cut and Haulover, but Abie spent two years fishing out of Haulover more recently, and he had found some new spots that I didn't know about. So, in the course of the day we hit some of my spots and we hit some of his spots. We ended up with a really great catch of fish. We had a big ninety plus pound Warsaw grouper, a big red snapper, black groupers, amberjacks, just a whole cleaning table full of big beautiful bottom fish.

As we were cleaning up our catch in the afternoon, as always on the weekend especially, there were a lot of spectators standing on the dock. And I might add that all of our best catches that day came from Abie's secret fishing spots. In the crowd was a guy who was familiar with Captain Bouncer Smith, and he looked at our table of fish and said, "What a beautiful catch. Bouncer, you sure know all the secret spots to catch fish."

Abie and I still get a good laugh out of that on many occasions. We'll bicker back and forth whether we're on my secret spot or Abie's secret spot. Either way, Abie is a hell of a fisherman and an indispensable part of the crew.

Bill Mac Donald Full Moon Tarpon

I had a great client and friend back in the good old days named Bill Mac Donald. He loved tarpon fishing almost as much and I did. He chartered me to go tarpon fishing and it turned out to be a pretty good night. We caught three tarpon in quick succession using live shrimp in Government Cut. Bill said, "Doggone it, what a catastrophe."

I said, "What's that?"

He said, "We've got a bowling tournament tomorrow, and we're in first place. It's the end of the season, and it's the championship, and the tarpon are biting. Ah, the heck with the bowling, I'm going fishing."

I said, "You don't want to go tarpon fishing tomorrow night. Tomorrow is the full moon. The tarpon won't be biting. Once we get to the full moon they shut off."

I had a charter the following night so I went tarpon fishing and Bill went to his bowling championship, and sure enough they won their games. We had four or five tarpon that night and it was even better than the night before. When I talked to Bill the next day he said, "Doggone, you shouldn't have talked me out of it. By gosh I'm going tarpon fishing tonight. The heck with this championship."

I said, "Bill, it's the night after the full moon. They may have bit last night, but they can't bite again tonight. And you're in a position to win the championship. How can you abandon your team?"

He said, "Yeah, OK, you're right. I'll go finish off the championship – and those tarpon better not bite."

So we went out and had an epic night and caught seven or eight tarpon, and Bill won his championship. He was really happy with that, but he said, "Doggone, I can't believe you talked me out of going tarpon fishing again last night. I'm going tonight for sure."

So we were both out there that night, and neither one of us got a bite. So he missed this epic tarpon bite and when he finally got to go, the fish turned off. That's how fishing works.

What generally happens is that before the full moon the tarpon get thicker and thicker because they're grouping up to go offshore to spawn. Then, on the full moon, they all go twenty miles out into the Gulf Stream to spawn. When they have done that they come back a couple of days later. What I had forgotten was that in January and February the fish aren't spawning yet so the full moon disappearance of fish doesn't take place. So I had talked Bill into not going for a couple of nights and they bit like crazy because they were still there. It wasn't time to spawn yet. I really put my foot in my mouth on that one, but thank goodness he at least won the bowling tournament.

Anchored for Triggerfish and Remora

I was out fishing on a Saturday morning and we had people from TR1 Autopilots out with us. It was a very crowded weekend; there were boats all over the place. There was a tournament going on that we weren't fishing. We anchored on a couple of spots and had an epic day. We had blackfin tunas, and black groupers, gag groupers, mutton snappers, cobia, and a few kingfish, just a really great day, especially eating fish.

All throughout the day people would call me on the radio and ask what we were catching. I was anchored, and I would be giving away our fishing spots if I told people exactly what we were catching. So I would answer that we were catching a bunch of ocean tallies, and remoras, and triggerfish. I threw in a couple of kingfish or bonitos here and there, but nothing truthful about what we were catching. I just couldn't tell people that here we were catching groupers and snappers and cobia. I wanted to maintain the integrity of our good bottom spots, or else everybody else would fish them and they would get wiped out.

At the end of the day we returned to the dock and unloaded our catch and piled it all up on the cutting table. It was piled high with all these nice fish, and along came Joe Turner and Leo Lombera down the dock. They were fishing this tournament and they came over and stood by our cutting table. Joe said, "That's a hell of a catch you've got there, Bouncer. Just which ones are triggerfish and which ones are remoras?"

We all had a good laugh, and we still laugh about it once in a while. I'll be kind of quiet on the radio and Joe will call me to ask if I'm catching triggerfish or remoras or what. But we saved our secrets till the end of the day and caught a lot of fish and had a lot of fun.

McClellanville

Around 1974 or 1975 a man contacted me to deliver his forty-foot Viking from Ft. Lauderdale to Atlantic City, New Jersey. He was a retired police sergeant from New York City, and one of his son's friends, a young man by the name of Larry, was going to ride along with me. We left out of Ft. Lauderdale the first day and ran up the ocean quite a ways. We chose to go on the inside around Cape Canaveral. But we got stuck at a railroad bridge and this set us way behind schedule.

That first day of our trip was Larry's birthday and we had planned to go out to dinner to celebrate. But we got to New Smyrna Beach too late to go out to dinner. The marina where we planned to tie up and get fuel was locked up tighter than a drum. We could get off the boat and walk around the marina, but we couldn't get out of the marina to go out to dinner. So we made dinner on the boat. The next night was my birthday so we agreed that we would have a birthday dinner at Thunderbolt, Georgia.

We left out of New Smyrna Beach, but were unable to get fuel there because they didn't open early enough. We took off headed for Thunderbolt, just below Savannah. We really pushed our luck I guess because going into Thunderbolt we ran out of fuel on one engine. So we crept into this 'in and out' storage marina just inside the inlet and tied up the boat. Talk about bugs, it was so buggy that we could hardly run out, hose the boat off, and run back in and close the door. Once again, two days in a row, and now it was my birthday and we were locked up in this 'in and out' storage marina closed up for the night. So we had to cook again on the boat, but these were very simple not extravagant dinners. I don't remember what we made, but it wasn't much. Anyway, we ate dinner on the boat again. We got fuel in the morning, got the engine primed, and took off again.

Now we were falling behind on our schedule of planned stops. I had been studying the Yachtman's Guide to the Intracoastal Waterway, and it had a whole page ad about McClellanville Marina and Skipper's Chowder House in South Carolina. Half the page was the marina and half the page was the restaurant. It really intrigued me. It was about thirty or forty miles north of Charlestown, and it was an easy day's run for this day, so we went in Charleston Harbor and went up the Intracoastal Waterway. It was all lowland swamps. As far as the eye could see to the east and west was swamp grass. We would pass hammocks of live oaks occasionally on either side of the waterway, but it was a very desolate area. We finally came to the channel marker for the side creek to go to the McClellanville Marina. We turned up there and started running into shrimp boats. I had read all about this big fancy McClellanville Marina and expected to see 300 boats or so. We got there and it was one long straight dock parallel to shore, probably 400 feet long. We were the only boat there as we pulled up to the fuel dock. The proprietor came out and said we could spend the night there and we wouldn't have to move. He was getting ready to go home. So we were fueling up the boat and Larry was down taking a shower. The proprietor came out and asked if we were going to Skipper's Chowder House. I said, "Yeah, we sure are."

He said, "Well, I'm going to call and tell them you're coming because they're getting ready to close up. I'll tell them to wait for you. How many of you are there?"

I said, "There's just the two of us."

He said, "OK, I'll tell them to wait for you."

I finished fueling the boat and asked, "How do we get to Skipper's Chowder House?"

The proprietor said, "Well, you go down this street and when you come to the third house, go between it and the fourth house, cut through the yards and you come out on the next street. If you'll look to your right you'll see a yellow flashing light at the intersection, and the place is across the intersection on your left.

So we got cleaned up in a hurry because the restaurant was getting ready to close. When we went down the street and went between the houses and came out the other side, a collie greeted us on the other side. This collie was barking her head off and escorted us all the way to Skipper's Chowder House, barking as we went along – not threatening, just keeping her distance and barking at us.

We walked up to the front door of the restaurant and could see people in there eating, but the door was locked. So we went around to the right and found another door, and it too was locked. We went around to the back and found an open door there so we went in, kind of down the side of the kitchen, down a hallway, around a corner, around another corner, down a hallway, and we came to what appeared to be a foyer entrance to the restaurant. Sure enough, this was the entrance. We had gone three quarters around the building and the main entrance was on the next side of the building. The reason the entrance was on the west side of the building instead of the front of the building was because they couldn't serve alcohol if the entrance was a certain distance from a church. Therefore they had to use this side entrance because the front door was too close to the church.

We were only going to be there once, but we learned our lesson on how to get into Skipper's Chowder House. We sat down to dinner and along came Aunt Jemima, a big heavyset African American lady. She asked to take our order, so we looked over the menu and made our choices. I know that mine included asparagus because of how fresh it was. The dinner was very good too. Then Aunt Jemima came over again to take our dessert order. I ordered pecan pie and Larry looked over the menu and ordered apple pie. Well, she didn't bring us individual slices of pie; she brought us each our own whole pie. They were something like four inches in diameter, but boy were they good. It was a meal fit for a king.

It was really neat. I asked her about making a phone call because I wanted to check in with my wife. She told me to just go there into the library where there was a phone. So I went in there, and honest to goodness, the phone was on the wall. It was the kind where you take the handset off the wall and click the hangar for the handset, and the operator answered so I could place my call like something out of Mayberry RFD. I told my wife that everything was going well. But what a birthday dinner we had there in McClellanville.

So we got on the way, again and in North Carolina we were going to pick up the owner of the boat and a couple of his sons. We had been traveling three days already and had one more day before we were going to pick up the owner.

Miami was still a small town back in those days, nothing like it is today. But about New York I had this impression of all

85

the crimes that were going on in New York based upon the TV shows that I watched. The whole way I was constantly grilling Larry about the trials and tribulations and dangers of living in New York City. And he would keep telling me it was no big deal.

We picked up the retired police sergeant and his two sons in Wrightsville Beach, NC. Obviously at some point Larry told them about my curiosity about the crime in the city. We eventually got to Atlantic City and went to the Casino, and boy, what a disappointment that was. I had always visualized casinos as you saw them on TV with women in beautiful evening gowns and gentlemen dressed in suits and sports coats in really high class places. We went into these casinos and here's an old man with his shirt unbuttoned and cigar ash laying all over his bare stomach. Women in shorts and t-tops, with the muffin top sticking out over their shorts, playing the slot machines. It was such a disappointment after all the respect I had for casinos to see what really went on there. It turned out they just load busses up in the major cities within a bus ride of the casinos and bus the people in there. It was far from what I expected.

But at any rate, the next morning we got up. We had a rental car and we drove to New York City. As we approached the city the sergeant said, "I'm going to show you all five boroughs so you can be familiar with New York."

So he took me to all five boroughs, and every ten or fifteen minutes somebody would shout out, "Oh, there's a mugging; oh there's a robbery." This happened throughout all five boroughs and we ended up in Queens where the sergeant lived and we went down to where one of the sons had a bar called The Vault. The bar was in an old bank building. We had a few drinks there and in short order they took me to the airport and sent me on my way.

What a fantastic first trip to bring a boat up the east coast of the United States with all the trials and tribulations, but great memories of a fantastic trip to Atlantic City and then driving on up to New York.

Caicos Island Bonefish

Peter Bakwin was a very wealthy Chicago resident who owned a mother ship named *Taurus* that he kept predominantly in Miami. On the mother ship he had two bonefish skiffs and a twenty-foot center console Mako. He would sent *Taurus* anywhere he heard there was potential for good bonefish action, and any other kind of action. He would bring his guests down to the mother ship and take them out bone fishing or for whatever seemed right for the time and place.

Mr. Bakwin read a story in Saltwater Sportsman Magazine about the writers catching eighty-three bonefish in one day in South Caicos. He absolutely loved bone fishing, so he had to go to South Caicos to check out this action. The *Taurus* operation had a captain, and a mate, and an engineer, and a stewardess/chef, but they always hired a fish mate to take care of the fishing operations wherever they went.

At the time they were looking for a fish mate and Pflueger Taxidermy introduced me to the captain. We arranged it so they would take the boat down to South Caicos and I would fly in on a DC-3 supply run to the island and meet them there. I would explore the fishing for a couple of days before Mr. Bakwin and his guests got there, and then I would be in charge of fishing operations off the boat.

I flew down to South Caicos and boarded the boat. I took the Mako and explored the options for reef fishing. They had arranged for a local bone-fishing guide to show us where to go. There was this immense tackle room on board *Taurus* to work with. It had boxes and boxes of spinning reels, rods, bone fish jigs, fly rods and flies, anything anyone would need for any kind of fishing from pin fish all the way up to blue marlin. I undertook the project of getting everything ready for the first day of bone fishing.

We had four guests including Mr. Bakwin, and my good friend Jerry Webb, and a couple of other fellows. One the first days of fishing I ran into town and picked up the bonefish guide and brought him back to the mother ship. We had the two boats ready to fish. Four guests came down, two in each boat, and we headed off to the bonefish grounds. The native guide led us onto these great big white flats. He stopped and said, "You guys work your way downwind from here, and we'll go over a half mile and parallel you, and we'll check back with you in an hour."

I had two guests on my boat as we were polling down the flats. We didn't see a crab, or a cowfish, or a shark, a bonefish, nothing. It was like a big sand desert. So after more than an hour the native guide and Mr. Bakwin came back and asked, "You guys have any luck?"

"Nope."

The guide said, "OK, then go down here a ways or so." We ran across the flats for a few more miles and he said, "You guys work down that way, and we'll go over there and work down that shoreline, and we'll check back with you in an hour."

So I was polling down this beautiful white sand desert with no life, and the other boat was along the shoreline polling along, and we didn't see them doing anything. An hour later they ran over to us and, "You see anything?"

"Nope."

"You catch anything?"

"Of course not."

Mr. Bakwin turned to the guide and said, "We heard about catching eighty-three bonefish in a day. Where are the bonefish?"

And the guide said, "Well, I got a spot we can try." So, we took off running again and pretty soon we were running in this beautiful little mangrove-lined channel to where it joins the ocean. We went around the bend and the guide stopped right next to a deep hole. He said, "This is where they caught the eighty-three bonefish, in this deep hole."

The guide and I each give our guests bucktails. They bounced the bucktails in the deep holes, but still nothing bit. We tipped our bucktails with shrimp and they started bouncing these in the holes, but still no bites. I rigged up a rod with a hook with a shrimp and a split shot and let it settle in the hole; still no bites.

Mr. Bakwin said to the native guide, "This is where the magazine writers said they caught eighty-three bonefish?"

The guide said, "Yeah, Mon."

He asked, "Where are the bonefish today?"

"I don't know, Mon. Yesterday we net this hole, it was full of bonefish. We caught hundreds of bonefish in our net. I don't know why there's no bonefish today."

The answer was that they had netted all the bonefish the day before, and that's why there were no bonefish on the flats or anywhere. The natives came while at low tide and netted them all and we were trying to catch fish in the dead sea.

We did end up with a pretty successful trip. The native guide and Mr. Bakwin would leave the *Taurus* in the morning, and the guide and the captain would agree where they were going to meet in the afternoon. We would blue water fish around the Caicos Islands to where we were supposed to meet the native guide, and we would spent the night in the mouth of a creek. Then we would get up in the morning and take off bone fishing, and work our way around blue water fishing. We eventually worked our way around to Provo on the west end of Caicos. In so doing we caught some blue marlin and yellowfin tuna. We had really nice fishing, and the bonefish boat caught a few bonefish everyday, mostly working muds, and mostly catching smaller fish.

The bonefish guide saved the flats day for bone fishing, and the captain and I saved the day for everybody else. Everybody ended up having a really great trip to the Caicos Islands.

Floating Dreams

When you go offshore looking for mahi mahi, or any offshore fish really, one of the key things to look for is something floating in the water. I'm reflecting back on some things that have really rocked the boat for me with offshore floating debris. The abundance of debris floating offshore today is far less than the amount in years past. When I first started charter fishing offshore years ago, freighters used pallets and cranes to load their cargo. Now it is all containerized freight, so there are no more pallets and broken off boards and cargo nets, all the great debris we used to have to find dolphin. Unfortunately the one thing we see more of is smaller plastic debris like water bottles. Why fishermen throw water bottles, one-gallon water jugs, chum boxes, and other things we see day after day makes me scratch my head.

Something else we see a lot of today is Mylar balloons. The cruise ship industry gets all the blame, but in reality, in Southeast Florida, those balloons more likely came from a party in Orlando, or Alabama, or it might even come from Ohio depending on how the jet stream is running. Those balloons go way up into the upper atmosphere and when the prevailing winds are to the southeast they carry the balloons out over the ocean, and then the balloons lose their lift and settle back down on the water. Maybe if we could get that industry to print on the balloons where they came from we could control this, especially today when helium is at a scarcity and Mylar balloons are in abundance.

My good friend Robin told me the other day that when they go out in the Everglades they find lots of Mylar balloons. The last time I checked, those cruise ships could not get up into the southern Everglades, so I don't think they're the culprits.

Getting on to more attractive things, the first thing I think of is the day close to fifty years ago we searched offshore. I was running the *Top Luck* and we had not found anything offshore for hours. I finally found a barnacle covered two by four. I trolled by it knowing it had to have some mahi mahi under it, and lo and behold, as our bait skipped by it, up popped a 200 pound blue marlin. Now we knew why there were no mahi at that spot.

Probably the most amazing thing I ever found floating offshore was when I was with my good friend Al Hower. We found the bottom section of a fixed gear airplane. Now that was a scary one. This was the two wheels and probably eight feet of the belly of the airplane sticking up in the air. It was loaded with fish, and every time we got close to this airplane belly we would get attacked by ten to fifteen pound dolphin, or five to twelve pound rainbow runners. We caught a lot of fish there, but it was an eerie day because it was also a day when South Florida was totally engulfed in fog. Our visibility was probably about a half mile. I called the Coast Guard when I found the airplane and they agreed they needed to investigate and asked our location. I told them I thought we were somewhere around ten miles off Haulover Inlet but that we had very limited visibility. This was before the days of GPS, and we did not carry Loran, so I really could not give him a positive location. The conditions were so bad that they had a hard time searching, and there was no UPIRB signal that they could zero in on. So they gave up on trying to find the airplane, but it produced a lot of fish for Al Hower's guests and me.

The next really greater floater I think of was a tree that I spotted off in the distance. This was a big one, probably well in excess of 100 feet long and had branches all off the sides of it. I didn't get great detail on it because in four hours I never got to the tree. I could see it, but I never got to it.

It's kind of embarrassing today what we did that day. We filled our 151 fish box that extended all the way across the back of my boat. The fish box was full to the top. Then we pulled it a foot away from the back of the boat and filled in all the space behind it. Then we pulled it out a little farther and filled the space again. Finally I said, "Guys, we have got to go home." And this was not small fish. They were mostly fifteen to twenty-five pounders. The whole back of the boat was piled with dolphin. There were no cameras on the boat. There were no camera phones back then, and I usually didn't carry a camera, so this catch of dolphins has no pictures to remind us of how many we caught that day. It was amazing, and I kid you not, I was fishing that tree for four hours and I never got within a couple hundred feet of it.

A couple of other boats found us later that day and got in on the action. What a nirvana of a floater that was. We didn't get to where we do today when we exhaust the spot and put out a planer on a spoon or a diving plug and start catching wahoo. We never got to that, and we never got close enough to know if there were tripletails or almaco jacks or anything like that. Just nirvana of dolphin fishing.

One day I took my son out fishing. We were going to fish our way down to Elliott Key and camp out, and then fish our way back the next day and throw in a little diving as well. So we headed out during a time when there was a massive transfer of human life from Cuba to the United States, a big raft invasion. We ran out of Haulover Inlet and started heading southeast, and there we found a raft. We went over and caught a tripletail. Then there was another raft and we went over and caught a dolphin. Then three rafts in a row and we caught nothing. Then we caught a wahoo, and then some more dolphin, and then a couple more tripletails. It was not like looking for something to fish to; it was more like running from point A, to point B, to point C, just solid rafts all over the water. And it was all different types of rafts, big cubes of Styrofoam, inner tubes lashed together with wood, inner tubes just tied together. In them were jugs of water, picture albums, suitcases. What was happening was the Coast Guard would go from raft to raft as fast as they could, taking the people off and painting a big orange X on the raft so they would know the people had been removed. It was just a massive event. Our day of offshore running and gunning was quite successful, which was not like our evening of hanging out at Elliott Key.

I went in to one of the smaller side channels around Broad Creek. We anchored up, and put out a live pilchard. I fired up the grill as the sun started to set and, sure enough, a real big tarpon ate the pilchard. Terry fought that tarpon in and out of all these creeks and channels for a long time. He had a ball fighting it, and finally got it up close enough to the boat that I could grab the leader and pop it off and send it on its way. We went back and anchored up again and restarted the grill, and put out another pilchard. The boat was my fish around cuddy cabin Dusky, and while we were cooking dinner

95

and the sun was setting we hurried up to eat dinner while the mosquitos had their dinner too. That was not a desirable situation, so I pulled the anchor and ran out to the middle of the bay. That ran off most of the mosquitos, but in twenty or thirty minutes they found us again. It just became ridiculous. Between the mosquitos and the heat in the middle of August, finally in the middle of the night I upped anchor and ran back home and we got a decent night's sleep in our own beds. We had a great time running and gunning from raft to raft and catching that big tarpon, but we could have done without the heat and mosquitos to finish the day.

As to other floating stuff out there, I've encountered cargo nets all wadded up. I've caught loads of dolphin around them. I've come across sections of long line, where it would be bundled up and messed up in one spot, and which sometimes did, and sometimes didn't have dolphin on them. Then there were the good old pallets. I remember a time when we were fighting a blue marlin and, as we were fighting it, we went by a pallet that was surrounded by twenty to twenty-five pound dolphin. We were in the final throws of trying to catch this marlin so we didn't throw a bait to the dolphin. Shortly thereafter we lost the blue marlin so we went back looking for the pallet but couldn't find it.

That has happened to me swordfishing too. A big floater would go by just too far away for us to catch a fish off of it, and by the time we wound up our 1,800 depth line which is 2,500 or 3,000 feet of line, and we run north to look for the floater, it was nowhere to be found and we can't figure out how it disappeared. That's life in the big ocean.

One day I was running my old Dusky 256 out of Keystone Point Marina. I went offshore a ways from Haulover

Inlet, and found a freezer that had a shotgun blast in the middle of the side panel, and the door was gone off it. We caught seven or eight dolphin, all decent size schoolies, and went on our way. The next day I got on a plane and flew to Ocean City, Maryland. I was running a big Hatteras out of there, and lo and behold, one week after we found the freezer off Miami, I was eighty or ninety miles offshore of Ocean City, and there was this same refrigerator, same shotgun blast in the middle of the side, and five or six dolphin around it again. How about that for a coincidence, to find the same floater on two different occasions more than 1,000 miles apart.

There have been days when we were so desperate to find dolphin that we made a floater out of our boat. It can work, but the odds are against it. I still see people trying to do it today. They get on a weed line and put out some baits and just drift along and hope the dolphin will find them. It may happen from time to time, but it's a long shot.

Those are some stories about floating debris and some other side stories of what comes from it. One thing for sure, when you head out offshore, always keep a sharp eye out. If it's not surrounded by dolphin it might have some tripletails around it, so you can throw little pilchards or live shrimp out to them. Also be ready with a deep diving plug or a planer with a plug on it. If you have to, go by it several times, because with that deep diving lure you really have a chance to catch a wahoo. Whatever it is, give it your best shot and keep going offshore looking for that floating debris.

Richard Fitzer Shrimp Theory

There was a time when we were convinced that if you want to catch tarpon off Bal Harbor you had to use mullet. I was out there one day with Larry Able and Richard Fitzer fishing with live mullet, but we couldn't get a bite. We had a couple of bites in the morning, but now it was mid afternoon and there were plenty of tarpon around, but there was nothing we could do to get them to bite. We started to fish just trying to catch a blue runner or anything.

I had some shrimp left over in the live well from a bonefish trip the day before, so I grabbed a spinning rod and hooked on a shrimp and threw it out behind the boat. There was a lot of seaweed around and we caught some on one of the mullet. I laid down the spinning rod while Larry wound in the mullet and I took the seaweed off. I cast the mullet back out and the same time we almost lost the spinning rod overboard because a tarpon ate the shrimp and took off running. I grabbed the spinning rod in the nick of time, but we lost the tarpon. We re-baited with a live shrimp again and caught another tarpon.

It was the beginning of a great run forty, maybe fifty years of using live shrimp for tarpon. One interesting story that came out of it: Larry Able owns his own Aquasport, and his number one fishing buddy was Richard Fitzer. The nice thing about the tarpon is you can go after work. So Larry and Richard would go to Fred Lou Bait and Tackle to buy their live shrimp. Larry would go in and say, "Give me two dozen hand picked shrimp." Regular shrimp were a buck and a half a dozen, and hand picked shrimp were three dollars a dozen. So Larry would get one and a half or two dozen live shrimp. Richard Fitzer was on a very tight budget, so he would say, "Give me a dozen and a half of the biggest shrimp that aren't hand picked. So Fred and Louise would sort through the shrimp, and not give him the biggest, but they would give him some pretty good sized shrimp. Then Larry and Richard would go tarpon fishing at night.

Night after night Richard caught more tarpon than Larry did, and I started paying attention to that. I started avoiding the very biggest shrimp and began using the medium shrimp for tarpon bait. And consistently these shrimp got a lot more action than the handpicked shrimp. Good-sized shrimp produced more tarpon than the bigger shrimp. I think it all came from the shrimp gliding through the water. That became the Richard Fitzer Tarpon Shrimp Theory, and it has worked ever since.

My First Hunt

When I was a really small young lad in Michigan my dad shot a big buck with a bow and arrow from across the stream. The buck ran up a hill and across a field. My dad crossed the stream and went up the hill and discovered acres of red ground cover. It made it impossible to track this big buck that he knew he had killed. He never found the buck, and I know it just made him feel sick. When he got home his arrows were all broken in half and he never hunted again. Therefore I never got exposed to hunting as I was growing up.

When I was in high school I was a regular on Sunny Isles Fishing Pier. A father and son invited me to go dove hunting with them. So I went with them one afternoon and went through two boxes of shells, but no doves were injured in my attempts at dove hunting. I never tried to hunt again until my sixty-fifth birthday. I had developed an interest in all that I heard about hog hunting. One of my best friends, Matt Tambor, was real into hog hunting. He had been doing it for a little over a year and was really enjoying it. So I expressed to him about a month before my birthday how much I would love to do it.

Sure enough, as my birthday approached, he said we would go hunting. It was all set up. I was to be at his house at four o'clock in the morning or something like that, maybe even three thirty. So we got in his truck and drove out Alligator Alley. About half way across we took Snake Road up toward Lake Okeechobee. We came to a turnoff into some rustic woods, and finally came up to an open development. There was a bunkhouse there and two gentlemen, the ranch owner and the hunting guide named Rick. They were preparing a great big country breakfast. My gosh, we had steak and eggs, and biscuits and everything a guy could want for breakfast. Rick took Matty over and dropped him off at a blind. Then he came back and picked up Tyler Tambor and me and put us in his hunting buggy, which was like a portable hunting blind. It was a gasoline driven golf cart. We went across the cattle ranch and through thickets and around turns. Finally we drove across a clearing and put the buggy right up against a big pile of brush. He told Tyler and me to get up in the back seat, which was elevated even more so we could see over the pile of brush. He took a bucket of corn and dumped it all over the ground. Then he came back and sat with us in the dark with an electric mosquito fogger. We waited for the sun to come up and the hogs to appear.

As we sat there in the dark, the sky started to lighten in the eastern sky, which was right in front of the buggy. Rick whispered to me to look over to my left and there were a half dozen deer feeding. Then a cow mooed, and a turkey gobbled, and songbirds began singing. Shortly thereafter Rick said that if we looked over to the right there was another bunch of deer. I looked over and there they were. The bucks were in velvet, and the does were all there; everybody having a great breakfast. It was quite boisterous with the cows mooing, the songbirds singing, and turkeys gobbling while we waited for the hogs to show up.

I was looking through the scope on the rifle and Rick was looking through binoculars and finally said, "Oh, some hogs have snuck in." There was a corn feeder hanging from a big oak tree that was set to go off at a certain time and spread corn all over the ground. The hogs were there waiting for it to go off. Then the feeder opened up and the hogs started feeding. I couldn't see them through the riflescope so he gave me the binoculars. But it was so dark in there and it was backlit besides, so I could barely make out the hogs.

Now there were turkeys all over the ground, and deer on both sides of our buggy, and cows all over the place. Suddenly this big black hog walked out of the dark over to where Rick had dumped this bucket of corn. Rick said, "Well, there you go. There's your hog. Now just line up right on the back of the shoulder there and fire when you feel confident." I was having trouble getting the sight lined up just right, and just when I got it a turkey was right where I was supposed to shoot.

I whispered over to Rick, "That turkey is right lined up with where I'm supposed to shoot. Shall I kill them both?"

He said, "No, no don't pull the trigger." This was an Osceola turkey and it's a $1,200 fine if you kill one of them. And it has to be in season. And it cannot be near a feeder, and a whole bunch of other rules. So he told me not to shoot, and the hog went back onto the darkness. Now the sun was coming up and there were turkeys all over the ground, and deer off to our left and right, and cows mooing. It was just the most beautiful morning; life as good as it gets. And here came the big black hog again over to the pile of corn. Rick said, "OK, there's your shot now. Let's get this hog."

So I lined the shot up and I was looking through the scope, and I saw the one I was supposed to shoot. The cows are mooing, and the turkeys are gobbling, and the songbirds are singing – deer to my left and deer to my right, and a hog lined up in my sight. I closed my eyes and pulled the trigger – BANG. The deer on my right and left disappeared. The turkeys stopped gobbling, the cows stopped mooing, and the songbirds shut up. The hogs disappeared. We got out of the vehicle and walked over to where the hog had been. There was no blood on the ground and no sign of anything being shot.

Rick said, "I was pretty sure you went under the hog or over the hog, one or the other, because I didn't think you hit him." Sure enough there was no wildlife around anywhere. That hunt was over.

But I'll never forget it. And later on in the day we found a big herd of hogs, but they were really out of range, and I came back with nothing. It took me a couple of more hunts before I got a hog, but that was one of the most phenomenal birthdays I ever had, and what a birthday present that was.

That hog hunt and everything about that day will be in my memory forever. Matt Tambor, and Tyler Tambor my cameraman, and Rick my guide, thank you so much for making that day so great.

Bait Eaters

Sometimes we have a problem with our baits and who eats them. One of my favorite stories is about a good friend of mine who ran a charter that originated in the Cape Canaveral area. He had a three-day charter in the middle of January with a man from Japan. The charter came to town and down to the marina. The captain meet with him and asked, "What would you like to catch over the next three days?

His charter answered, "Oh, I'm only here to catch sailfish. Sailfish or bust."

The captain slapped his forehead and said, "Man, there are no sailfish here this time of year. The sailfish are about 150 miles south of here."

The Japanese gentleman said, "Well, I wanted to catch sailfish. Is there anything we can do?"

The captain replied, "Well, if you'll charter us for another day, four days, the first day we'll run to Palm Beach, and then the next two days we'll fish for sailfish in that area, and go into Palm Beach each night. On the fourth day we'll fish for sailfish for a couple of hours and run back here to Cape Canaveral. "

The Japanese gentleman agreed, so they loaded up and ran down to Palm Beach and were all living on the boat. The captain and mate got up in the morning and had breakfast and got the boat ready. It was relatively calm so they figured to let the angler sleep because of the big time difference between Japan and Florida. They connected with a live bait boat, bought a dozen goggle eyes, and ran about ten miles north of Palm Beach Inlet to where the sailfish had been. The captain and mate were sitting up on the bridge because there was nothing left to do. The rods were all rigged and the outriggers were down. They were just waiting, shooting the breeze. They got to where they wanted to fish, the captain pulled back on the throttles, and the mate jumped off the bridge chair and ran down the ladder. The Japanese gentleman was sitting on the entrance to the salon wiping his face with a napkin. The mate looked into the live well, and it was empty. He was wondering 'what in the world has happened to all my goggle eyes?'

The Japanese gentleman looked up and said, "Oh, such a good breakfast, the sushi fish with the big eyes." The gentleman ate the whole dozen goggle eyes. So they turned around and ran back ten miles to Palm Beach and bought a couple dozen goggle eyes and went back out fishing. They had a successful two and a half more days of fishing, but they made it clear to the customer that the bait was not for breakfast. But they did make sure the customer had some kind of fresh fish for breakfast everyday. But what a mind blower to run 150 miles, buy the bait, go to the fishing grounds in the morning, and find that all the bait had been fileted and eaten by the one customer.

I had a similar situation one day when I was running a charter boat out of the Castaways Marina north of Haulover Inlet. Herbie was my mate, and my wife rode along. It was a hot summer Saturday morning and my wife was sitting up on the bridge with me. We were trolling along and we caught a small bonito, maybe five pounds. We trolled all down the coast but could not get a bite. So I called Herb up to the bridge and said, "Herb, take that bonito we caught, take the backbone out, put a big hook through the nose, put a couple of smaller hooks as trailers in the filets, and we'll troll it through the Cuda Hole. Let's see if we can at least catch these guys a big cuda."

Herb said, "Well, Bouncer, we have a problem with that."

I said, "What's the problem?"

He said, "We don't have a bonito."

I said, "Sure we do. We have that bonito we caught right after we started fishing."

Herb said, "Yeah, but our charter ate it about an hour ago." So, I was trying to upscale our catch by using our little fish to catch a bigger fish, but our little fish had been eaten raw by our charter.

One of my favorite situations that I see from time to time, and Abie gets really upset about it. But I can't say as I blame him because sometimes it's pretty upsetting to me too. We have a guy who eats our fresh fish on a regular basis when we want to use them for bait. For that reason he is our most unpopular dock guest. In case you haven't guessed, what happens is Abie gets to the dock bright and early in the morning, sets out the rods, cleans up the fish box, empties all the water out to get it ready for the new load of ice, and then takes the bonitos that he had stored in the fish box. He filets them out, cuts them down, and cuts beautiful strips out of these bonito filets, really primo baits for a day of fishing. Then maybe his phone rings, or something distracts him, and he has to leave the cutting table. As soon as he steps away from the table, these crested night herons that hang around the dock all the time jump up on the table and start eating his trolling strips as fast as they can. On more than one occasion they have completely wiped him out of trolling strips. Plenty of times he has had to chase them off as they were gobbling down his baits.

His most concerning day was the time he was rigging mono leader ballyhoo at the cutting table and turned to go get a skirt or something, and a beautiful big white egret ate a trolling ballyhoo - hook, leader, and all. Abie chased it all around the marina trying to catch up with it so he could at least cut the leader off close to its mouth. That egret got away and we never saw it again. I sure hope he figured out a way to survive it. We really love our marina guests, the big white egrets, great blue heron, our crested night herons. We have female black birds that come down to our cutting table every afternoon that we hand feed. Of course we have all of our tarpon and nurse sharks that we cater to as well. We live in a great atmosphere and it's really funny how our baits are eaten in unexpected ways.

Government Cut Seamount

About six or seven years ago they were going to dredge Government Cut from forty-six feet to fifty-two feet to facilitate the new super freighters coming from Asia. When they were getting ready to dredge Dan Kipnis was on the panel to oversee the dredging operation. He said if they were going to dredge there was going to have to be a benefit directly, therefore all dredge materials must be dropped on the exact GPS coordinates offshore.

This was done. We watched them do it. We would see the tugs with the barges coming offshore and dumping the fill. Now we knew from a project twenty-five years ago that these rock piles would eventually produce fish. But this time they were out to build a seamount. They successfully built the seamount in 450 feet of water and the pile of fill came all the way up to 325 feet. I just knew it was going to be a fish producer.

They might not have been done dumping fill when we caught an almaco jack dropping on this new seamount. When they were done we started going there regularly, and boy, it was so good. We caught amberjacks up to seventy-five and eighty pounds. We caught blackfin tunas, and almaco jacks up to thirty-five pounds. We could go there any day. We could be having a bad day with nothing biting, but we could go to the seamount and catch a big fish for everybody on the boat. Then we started catching these snappers and blackfin tunas, and the neat thing about it was that we frequently didn't use any bait. We did a lot of heavy vertical jigging with heavy spinning reels with fifty-pound braid. On the end of it we would have a skinny Williamson vertical jig. We could drop it to the bottom and jig it up as fast as we could and the people would be catching these beautiful fish up to seventy-five pounds, just having a ball. And the great thing about it was that for a couple of years only two boats ever went to the seamount. Captain Wayne Conn would bring his Reward there with his troops of people, and we would go there. Nobody else ever fished this seamount.

Well, all good things must come to an end. Eventually a couple of people figured out what was going on there and they came across it in their travels. They started snapper fishing and jack fishing as well. Then the sharks were attracted by this heavier boat traffic. Now, unfortunately, you can go there and hook a big fish, maybe a big grouper or more likely some kind of big amberjack, or almaco jack, and almost every one of them will be eaten by a shark. There are boats there everyday, all day long with electric reels hauling up whatever snappers they can catch. It just isn't like it used to be.
But what a great memory of a secret spot that gave us and our clients a couple of years of great fun.

Strange Encounters

People often ask me the craziest things I have seen in fishing. The list goes on and on. The first one that comes to mind was back in my Castaways days when I was running a small Norseman, which had been run in the past by Ronnie Schatman. Ronnie was an avid shark fisherman, and he had filled a huge chest freezer in the main salon with shark baits, and pieces of sharks including unborn juvenile sharks. The boat went to the boatyard and was tied up for a while, so Ronnie quit the boat while it was laid up. Somehow, while the boat was being worked on, the 110 power was unplugged and it was left without power. Sure enough, here was this freezer full of unfrozen shark parts and bait. When the boat came out of the yard I was hired to run the operation. The first chore I had to take care of was solving this problem of this freezer full of absolutely disgusting, stinky slush. To keep from having to smell and breathe the dead, rotten fish, I wore a mask and scuba tank. I used a five-gallon bucket to dip the disgusting slime out of the freezer into the bucket, and carry it out and dump it over the side. I did this over and over and over again.

It was a warm summer day and I got warn down, so I took a break and climbed up on the dock with the boat's owner and a couple of other fellows. This slick of yuck was floating down the canal away from the north side of the Castaways docks. Lo and behold, this really sharp fin cut through my chum line. My response in my mind was 'What was that?' It was sharp like a jack crevalle's tail, but it was way too long to be that. I couldn't imagine what it was. About that time there was some splashing and thrashing where the riprap of the parking lot met the concrete seawall at the entrance of the west side of the hotel.

The *Bandit* was tied up nearby and a couple of its crewmembers ran over to where the thrashing was and started hollering that it was a sailfish. As the sailfish swam down that seawall and passed alongside the *Bandit*. One of the crewmembers on board reached out a long handled gaff, free gaffed the sailfish, and pulled it into the boat. Skip Rudolph was one of the crewmembers who pulled it into the boat. They had a great debate over who was going to have it mounted. This was back when taxidermists used the bill, the tail, some fins, and stretched the skin over the sides to make a mount. They decided that someone would get a real tail in the mount, another would get a real bill, and they would each get one side of the skin. This sailfish swam two miles up the Intracoastal Waterway north of Haulover Inlet and back to the east nearly a half-mile to reach the location where it met its demise alongside the *Bandit*. So that was a really crazy event.

Another crazy thing happened while I was running a boat out of Bahia Mar in Ft. Lauderdale. Bob Raulerson was my mate at the time. We were fishing in a couple hundred feet of water off Port Everglades. We had a live pinfish in the right short rigger looking for anything we could use for shark bait. This long black and slinky sea monster (and today I still don't know what it was) came after that pinfish. As the creature was trying to grab the pinfish, Bob was so scared by it that he

111

yanked the pinfish right out of the water, and the Denison of the Deep disappeared. We'll never know what it was, but who knows? It was long and black and ugly, and it's still out there to attack another pinfish another day.

Another event happened with some Englishmen who came over and chartered me quite often. They would generally fish for a week or more. One part of the group would fish for tarpon and sailfish and sharks, while the rest of the group would go bone fishing and permit fishing on the flats. On this particular day my group was offshore sail fishing, but there was nothing biting. So we came into Government Cut to try for tarpon. We were slow trolling live mullet all along the south side of the Cut to no avail. As we were trolling along the tip of the south jetty a sailfish came after my mullet. He chased it but he wouldn't eat it. It was a fairly small sailfish and a pretty big mullet, but they never made final contact. I searched back through the area several times but never saw the sailfish again. Nothing was biting so we wound them up and went into Miami Beach Marina to grab some lunch. After lunch we headed back out the Cut, and what did we see at the tip of the north jetty? A gentleman with a yoyo in one hand and a sailfish in the other. He had been fishing off the end of the rocks and caught a sailfish on his hand line. Possibly the same sailfish, we'll never know for sure. But that was the one that got away without even biting the bait, but makes a story that has lasted for years.

Several years ago everyone was catching herring all the way in by the Coast Guard base at Miami Beach Marina, and one of the boats spent the an hour and a half or two hours chasing a sailfish around in there. Every time it would pop up feeding on the herring they would run over and pitch it a bait, but they never could get it to bite.

112

It's amazing the travels that big game fish take. There was a 127 pound swordfish free gaffed at the Biscayne Bay Marriot when it first opened on the far west side of Biscayne Bay north of the Julia Tuttle Causeway. There were numerous sailfish and swordfish caught in Florida Bay. There was a school of bluefin tuna years ago that swam up into a residential canal in Cape Coral on the west coast of Florida. In the last couple of years there have been giant bluefin tunas and big swordfish nearly caught at the mouth of the channel going into Cape Florida. There was a blue marlin and a yellowfin tuna caught north of Peanut Island in Lake Worth years ago. The fish could show up anywhere, so you should always have the a variety of tackle rigged the right way to make it pay off.

Barry Karch

There was a time when business was slow for me. I had just moved back from the Keys and would do anything to stay busy. So I put signs up all over the place with business cards that said I would catch you more fish on your own boat. I was lucky enough that Barry Karch called me up one day and said he would like me to go on his boat that he kept in Little River off 79th Street. Barry had the Novi Iceland smoked salmon business in Little River. I met him at his boat and we went out fishing, but it was quite a fiasco. We fished all day, but I don't think we caught a fish. We tried everything under the sun. It was back in the olden days when we drifted with ballyhoo, we trolled, and we did some jigging on some wrecks, but nothing would work that day.

But Barry and I hit it off really well and we started fishing nearly every Monday. We would get on his boat and head out. We caught dolphin, and kingfish, and sailfish, a nice mixture of everything under the sun.

Barry called me up one day to tell me he had bought a brand new boat and invited me to go fishing on it the following Monday. I said, "Great, looking forward to it." So I went down on Monday and here was a nice Sea Ray, and the name on the boat was *Bouncer*. Barry had named his boat after me.

One of Barry's most memorable catches happened one day when I wasn't with him. He went live baiting and caught a hammerhead shark. Back then we had these things called Polaroid cameras. You would push the button and it would take a picture and spit the picture out of the side of the camera. You didn't have to take it to get it developed or anything. You could have your pictures instantaneously instead of having them a week later. So Barry hooked this hammerhead shark and pulled it up alongside his boat and pulled the rod up really hard to get the head up high. He pushed the button to take a picture, and the best he could guess was then when he picked it up really high, the line broke. The rod came back and nailed him right in the middle of the forehead. The next thing Barry knew was that something was pounding on the side of his boat. He crawled up off the deck and saw that he was up against the beach and there were people in the water holding onto his boat to keep it from going up on the sand. They were pounding on the side of the boat to wake him up. He had this big old knot on his forehead and he was there with his rod and reel with the line broken. There lying on the deck was a polaroid picture of a hammerhead shark. The rest of it is history, but it was an interesting thing.

One of the sidebars of dealing with Barry was at one point he had offered me a job opportunity. It was really tempting, but it would mean giving up fishing, and I just couldn't do it. He was on the ground floor of an industry that was going to take mullet, and menhaden, and croakers, and catfish, and they were going to put them in a spinning drum with steam. They were going to cook these fish down to nothing. This drum would have very small holes in it, and as it spun all of the cooked product would be forced out of the holes and be collected. It would be a liquid and then it would be dried down to a mush, and then they would reconstitute it using a starch to glue it together. Then they would add ten percent shrimp or crab flavoring and they would make artificial crab legs or shrimp, either one. I was going to be on the ground floor of running a factory making this reconstituted fish product. I chose to pass Barry up on that offer. I stuck to fishing and Barry stuck to smoking salmon, and for that matter smoking kingfish now and then for us. That crab product became quite famous for a while and artificial crab legs became the latest rage.

Barry Karch and I had some great times and I'll always remember Barry as a man who named his boat after me. Thank you Barry Karch for all the things we did together.

Cobia in Bimini

Marty Arostegui, whom I have mentioned many times in my stories, is a very generous guy. He was a member of the Miami Beach Rod and Reel Club and he had a Golden Rod on his Gold Badge. That's the highest level you can get in the Miami Beach Rod and Reel Club. David Harris was going for his Golden Rod on his Gold Badge, trying to catch up with Marty. One of the fish that he needed was an amberjack on fly. So the easiest way to catch an amberjack on fly is to find amberjacks on a wreck in shallow water where there is nothing near it but miles of sand. In Bimini we had numerous places that fit that bill perfectly.

So Marty Arostegui, David Harris, and I ran over to Bimini to go after amberjacks on fly. We went to the first wreck and there was a variety of fish, but no amberjacks. Then we went to the second wreck we call the Scarab. I was running the boat, and Marty was dropping the anchor, and David was waiting in the bow with his fly rod. I pulled up to the Scarab, which was a go-fast boat that was sunk about forty miles south of Bimini. When I thought we were lined up on the wreck I gave Marty the word to drop the anchor. I backed up to the wreck and Marty let out rope and tied us off.

I turned off the engines and looked back, and the whole bottom of the ocean rose up with a hundred cobias milling behind the boat. But we needed amberjack. So here we were, there might have been a hundred cobias, but only about four amberjacks. I would throw some chum to the right, and the hundred cobias and four amberjacks would rush to the right. David would try to throw the fly in front of the amberjack and he would have to snatch the fly out of the water right out of the lips of the cobia. Or he would be caught off guard and he would hook the cobia on the fly rod and have to land it. The first few we threw in the fish box, but then we started throwing them back. We would throw chum to the right and to the left and the amberjacks and cobias would follow it. David would throw his fly but the cobia would come up and chase his fly before the amberjack could get there.

Who would imagine that cobias could outrun amberjacks? But they would every time we threw chum in the water, and every time David threw his fly. It was the most unbelievable scene you ever saw when it came to cobias. Marty and David each caught cobia on the fly. I had never caught one on fly but I did now. When we prepared to leave four or five hours later, the cobias were still milling around behind the boat waiting for someone to throw in some chum or a fly. Either way the cobias were going to eat it and beat the amberjacks to the shot.

We went to another wreck and I can't be certain, but I think David caught his amberjack. But I do know that at the Scarab, there was no way to get an amberjack before a cobia ate the fly. It was a trip to never be forgotten.

Interesting note: on another occasion, Marty and I went to Bimini with his son, Martini. On this trip Martini wanted to catch a grouper. Marty was trying to encourage Martini to win some angling honors in the Rod and Reel Club and the Metropolitan South Florida Fishing Tournament, so we went to the same Scarab wreck. This time there were maybe a dozen cobias there, but they were much bigger cobias, and we immediately went to work on Martini catching them on different tackle. Martini and I were in one corner of the boat and I gave him a twelve rod with a bucktail. He was trying to catch the cobias on plugs while Marty was on the other side of the boat trying to hook a cobia on fly, but not having any luck.

Martini caught his cobia on plug, so then I gave him a spinning rod and he caught a cobia in the spin division. Then he caught a cobia with a pilchard on a bucktail on a plug rod, so that was a cobia on light tackle in general. Then he caught a cobia on a thirty-pound outfit with live bait, so that was cobia on heavy general. But Marty still could not catch a cobia on fly. He was switching rods, and switching flies, and now Martini was down to the only thing he needed: a cobia on fly.

I threw a couple of pilchards in the water and the cobia came after them. Martini threw the fly in the water and hooked one. The cobia was down below the boat, so Martini was leaning down over the side with the rod in the water and Marty said, "That fly doesn't work. Take this fly."

Martini and I turned around and in unison, "What are you talking about? We've already got a cobia on." So we caught the cobia on fly and eventually we left that spot because we had worn out the cobias. Martini had all of his line classes and tackle classes on fly and it was a really great start to our trip.

But remember, Martini wanted a grouper. So we ran to another wreck and anchored up there and Martini dropped a jig down to the bottom. He was jigging and jigging, trying to catch a grouper. He got a good strike and wound up with a big cobia. And he dropped down again, did the same thing, and came up with another cobia. We caught several fish on that wreck, cobias, mangrove snappers, big blue runners, and yellow jacks. We had a ball but no grouper.

We pulled up from there and ran to another wreck. This wreck was notorious because on numerous occasions we had caught two black groupers on one plug at the same time. That's two fish on one plug with two treble hooks. And we had done that a couple of times. So we were there and Martini was trying to catch a grouper, and you guessed it, he caught more cobias at that wreck as well.

What a fabulous day of fishing. The good news, the next day we went out on the dropoff and Martini was deep jigging there and he did catch a big grouper. So all was not lost. He caught his grouper. He caught all of his cobia for all the line classes and tackle classes in the fishing competition. And that's great story about cobia fishing in the Bahamas. What a lot of fun.

Pflueger Supremes

When I became a teenager we were tired of catching all of our fish on spinning reels and were looking for a new challenge. So B.J. and Wayne Conn and I all bought Pflueger Supremes. These were direct drive reels with no drag. If the spool went around backwards, the handle went around backwards. The only way to slow a fish down was to put a thumb on the line, and that would get really hot in a hurry.

When we caught Spanish mackerel we took a little abuse. Our thumbs would get scorched. When the bonitos would show up at the pier we became the fastest thumbs in the west. We'd be holding the bottom of the rod below the reel, and with alternating hands we'd lick one thumb and put it down on the spool, and when it got hot we'd lick it and use the other thumb to hold the spool. Then we'd switch and lick, and switch and lick as these bonitos would be running off. Sometimes we would get a bucket of water to pour on the reel, and that's how we caught bonitos on the pier with our Pflueger Supremes.

Every bonito would run to the end of the spool as soon as it was hooked because, unlike on a boat where they can go around and around, on a fishing pier they just run straight offshore until the line runs out. The stretch of the line stops its forward progress and then we bring them back in. We melted some monofilament with our thumbs, and we melted some thumbs with our monofilament.

We got pretty good with our Pflueger Supremes for a wide variety of fish. We were the fastest crankers around, and would take these reels, which were relatively slow retrieves, and go out king fishing with one ounce nylon jigs with some Mylar strips on them. We would drop them down to the bottom and jig them up just as fast as we could. On my best trip I caught twenty-nine kingfish in a half a day. By the time I was done it was a polished, hammered jig head and a hook with some crinkly bent up wire attaching it to my line. There was nothing left of that jig head but raw lead with holes punched in it.

I caught several sailfish on a Pflueger Supreme. One of my all time greatest catches was when I was fishing on the *Seabreeze* with Captain Smitty. He had us over a ledge in 240 feet of water and I dropped a three-ounce bucktail down. I was jigging on the bottom and got a strike. I fought a fish up and you could hear me all the way up in Maine hollering, "It's a Warsaw." To this day and always this will be a Met record. The Met no longer exists and this Warsaw was caught on plug tackle with a revolving spool reel and artificial lure. It weighted twenty-seven pounds four ounces.

I've caught a lot of big amberjacks on Pflueger Supremes. In my other book I was talking about how I was casting for snook and how I got a terrific strike right at my feet from a monster snook. The drag only worked if you let off the handle, but I forgot to do that and the fish broke off. I put on another plug and did it again and broke off another big snook.

The fun that B.J. and Wayne and I had with those Pflueger Supremes will be remembered forever. The sad part about it is that after that model was no longer made I acquired a bunch of them from Al Hower who worked for Pflueger Tackle. I had a whole cooler full of them, but today I couldn't even tell you where they were. It's a shame that they are not around anymore. They sure made fishing challenging.

Dock Box Freddie

Early in my career when I was at the Castaways Docks, one of the characters I met, and became very good friends with, was Freddie Harvey, well known as Dock Box Freddie. When he was a kid and young man he literally lived in a dock box on Pier 5 in Miami. They had these dock boxes where they stored their spare paint and stuff like that. There was an empty box on the dock and Freddie started living in it. He worked on the charter boats, first washing them, and then progressed to become a mate, and then captain. He was very well respected as a fantastic bill fisherman, especially blue marlin. Freddie had a great love of alcohol that kept him run down most of the time. He was a great fisherman, but unfortunately had no other social life.

I got lucky enough to spend many a great day on the water with Freddie and I'll tell you what, he was so sharp that he could see a sailfish coming up on a trolling bait before the sailfish even saw the trolling bait. He was very knowledgeable about sailfish, blue marlin, and white marlin.

One of my favorite Dock Box Freddie stories was when the mullet run was going on in the fall. Freddie, and another captain, Gary Hall, and I decided to go tarpon fishing. We went out just to the south of Haulover Inlet where there was a big black school of mullet. Gary threw the net and he and I hauled it into the boat. Freddie drove the boat as Gary and I were putting the mullet into the live well. There were well over 100 all over the deck. We were picking them up, and if they were too big we would throw them back, and if they were a reasonable size we would put them in the live well.

Freddie hollered down from the bridge, "How long are you going to feed those tarpon before you start fishing?"

We looked behind the boat and here were these dizzy mullet swimming around. They had been on the deck depleted of oxygen, and they swam in crazy circles. The tarpon were exploding on them 100 yards behind the boat, so we quickly rigged some rods and put them out. But boy did those tarpon make fools out of us. It wasn't until later that we learned more about hooking tarpon, but that day a bunch of them jumped off the hook. I honestly believe that we landed perhaps one tarpon for about forty strikes.

But when you fish live mullet the strikes are just unbelievable. The mullet were there swimming on top of the water, and an eighty pound tarpon would come up and explode on the school. But he might miss. Then a hundred pound tarpon would come up from another direction and explode on the mullet and miss; then it's a sixty pounder, then a 150 pounder. The mullet were scrambling to get out of the way as the tarpon jumped in the air, and finally one of the tarpon would nail a mullet and take off running and jumping. It's always a sight to behold.

But getting back to Dock Box Freddie who was just a fantastic friend. We did so much fishing together back in the days when trolling sailfish was the ultimate way to go. He got stabbed in the lung one time, and we all had to take care of him for a few weeks while he recuperated. But through the years Freddie never got over his love of alcohol. Now he has moved on to that great fishing spot in the sky. But what a great guy he was, and he helped me learn so much about catching billfish.

Sharon's Smallest Fish

Every year for a couple of years my family, that was my sister, Sharon, and her husband, Todd, and my sister, Sue, and her husband, Joe, and I would join Allen Sherman for a charter in Flamingo in Everglades National Park. We would always have a second boat to fish Joe and Todd; and Sue, Sharon, and I would fish with Allen.

One year was a total fiasco. It was the coldest day of the year. Fishing was absolutely terrible. I think the fish were all frozen. The highlights of the day were Sharon caught a catfish, and she also snagged Sue. Sue has red hair. So when we got back to the boat ramp and met with the guys, Allen and I, and Sharon and Sue all swore that Sharon caught a big red. Sue went home and photo shopped Sharon's rod bent over and on the end of her line a redfish. So for a long time we had the guys convinced that we did catch a redfish on the coldest day of the year in Flamingo.

Another time we went with Allen Sherman and the weather was much nicer. We were fishing up in Snake Bight. I was fishing in the stern of the boat, Allen was just forward of me at his helm station, and the two girls sat on the front bench facing forward fishing off the bow. The girls were using bobbing corks, actually Cajun Thunders. Allen was baiting them with shrimp. He would spot cast their baits to where he thought they would have the best chance. They would sit there and make their Cajun Thunders rattle and hope for a bite. It wasn't real good fishing, just a couple of small fish. Sharon wound in her line and Allen took off her shrimp and put on a little tiny pilchard. He threw that out there and handed the rod back to Sharon.

Sue and I always made a thing about who caught the smallest fish. Allen said, "OK, we're going to leave this spot, so let's wind them up." So I wound in my artificial lure. Sue wound in her live shrimp, and Sharon came in with this little tiny pilchard on her hook, and she was swearing up and down that she had caught the smallest fish. The fact of the matter was, and we had the hardest time convincing her, I might add, that she was really using a tiny pilchard for bait and that fish on her hook was actually her bait.

The day improved as we went along. We moved out to the west a little bit and got into some good trout action, and some real good shark fishing. Sue caught a big bull shark, and it turned out to be a great day. The guys on the other boat did catch some snook, and sea trout, fishing with Pete Salot.

Everybody had a good time. And those were some great times fishing with Allen Sherman in Flamingo.

Canadian Captain Kangaroo

When I was a kid I went out fishing with my dad and his buddies on a charter boat out of the Castaways Motel. My dad built rods, among other things, and by the time we went out on this charter boat we had been fishing for years, usually on my dad's boat fishing for dolphin. When we got into a school of smaller fish we would pull out our light spinning rods and have a ball catching these schoolie dolphin.

So my dad chartered this boat to take his good friend out after a blue marlin off Miami Beach. We unloaded out of the car, and Dad grabbed a handful of light spinning rods and went down to the boat. As we came aboard the mate asked what we thought we were going to do with those. My dad replied that he knew we were going blue marlin fishing but there was a good chance we would run into some dolphin too.

The mate replied, "Well, you can put those up in the front cabin and we'll see about that."

We didn't see any blue marlin that day, but we caught some schoolie dolphin on fifty-pound test on heavy boat rods. We caught some nicer dolphin on trolling equipment, but the little spinning rods stayed up in the front cabin at the mate's direction. My dad was not at all happy about it either. Schoolie dolphin on big game tackle was not really that much fun.

Later on my wife and I decided to go to Ocala to go large mouth bass fishing trying to catch a really big bass. When I booked the guide on the telephone I asked what kind of tackle I should bring. I was told not to bring tackle, and that they would have everything we would need. I replied that I really liked to use my own stuff, so it was suggested that I bring my rods and reels, but with no line on them and they would supply us with the line the guide likes to use. So we went up the day before the trip, and at the tackle shop we were told that the guide only uses this blue Stren line. At the tackle shop it cost about twelve dollars to fill a Pflueger Supreme with their line. Fifteen-pound Ande would have cost about two dollars. At any rate, I filled my reel with their glowing blue Stren line.

We got up at five in the morning and came to the boat. I was there with my Pflueger Supreme and a popping rod. The guide walked out and asked what I was going to do with that. I said that's what I liked to fish with. The guide was skeptical and indicated we would see about that.

We bass fished all day using conventional reels with seventeen-pound Stren and popping rods. But, "Oh, no. Your rods won't work."

I said, "I think they will." Back and forth disagreeing. But we didn't catch any big bass, and I didn't get to use my rod. But from that lesson I realized the value of respecting a client's fishing tackle.

So now, a few years later, I was down at Bud and Mary's in Islamorada guiding on a flats skiff. This fellow booked me for a day of tarpon fishing. He came down to the boat with a big spin casting reel on about a fifteen-pound class spin casting rod, which is a spinning rod turned upside down. I asked, "You hoping to fish with that?"

He said, "Yeah, I sure hope so."

I said, "Well, I've never used a spin cast like this. Are they pretty durable?" My understanding was they didn't have rollers on the rod and stuff like that.

He said, "Yeah, I catch all my fish on that."

We went down to Channel Five Bridge and were fishing with live mullet. The first place I anchored up had some real big cudas. We caught a cuda on my heavy outfit, and then we tried to catch one on his rod, but every one we hooked broke the line. We caught a couple more barracudas on my twenty-pound spinning rod. Then we filled his reel up with twenty-pound test and relocated to Channel Two Bridge. As soon as we pulled up, the big barracudas showed up. Now we had his rod filled with heavier line, so I rigged him up and we threw out a live mullet. A giant tarpon came up and crashed his mullet and took off running. With the twenty-pound line on his spin cast, it immediately ran out of line. The sheet metal reel seat on the handle collapsed and the reel popped off the reel seat and it went up the rod, bing, bing, ping, bing as all the guides popped off his rod. He was left standing there with a fiberglass stick with a cork handle and nothing else, no guides, no reel, nothing. I couldn't help but laugh, as I had never seen anything like that happen.

So we went back to using my tackle and when we got back to Bud and Mary's that night he bought a nice brand new Shakespeare fishing outfit filled up with twenty-pound test that he could fish the rest of his trip with. And we started having some really good times.

It turned out that he was the Captain Kangaroo equivalent from Canada. And he was a really nice guy. We had a great time catching a bunch of barracudas and tarpon. But I'll never forget the spin cast going bing, bing, bing, bing – splash, off into the distance. That was a good one.

131

Julian Galan's Free Jumping Sailfish

Free jumping sailfish. Now, what's that all about? Well, let me start back in the early days. My dad and I built a boat in the very early sixties, and one day we took his best friend from Michigan, Julian Galan, out on the boat. It was slick glass calm and we were drifting somewhere south of Haulover Inlet in about 120 feet of water. A sailfish came up and jumped right off the bow of the boat. Julian said, "Where's my camera. I've got to get a picture of that."

My dad said, "It won't jump again."

So Julian headed back to his fishing rod, but the sailfish jumped again. So Julian took off for his camera but my dad said, "Don't bother." And Julian headed back to his rod; and the fish jumped again. This sailfish jumped all the way around the boat, probably twelve or fifteen jumps. And Julian never got his eight-millimeter camera out of its carrying case to take a video of it. But he got it out when the jumps were all over, and we never saw another free jumping sailfish again that day.

So, what's the story with these guys? Well, my opinion, which is shared by a lot of people, is that we know that sailfish get these small remoras three or four inches long sticking onto their bodies. Our thinking is that when these remoras work their way up into the gills they irritate the sailfish so they jump to dislodge the remoras from their gills. They're obviously not feeding because when they jump they land flat on their sides. They'll jump four or five times in rapid succession and then they'll disappear.

For years we just took this to be a sideshow and say, "There's a jumping sailfish, isn't that nice." About 1970 I saw a jumping sailfish and I turned over toward it, and lo and behold, sailfish showed up behind every bait we were trolling. We were trolling ballyhoo, and mullet, and teasers, and feathers. There were sailfish all over behind the boat. We managed to hook six and land five, which was unheard of back in those days, but what a thrill to have happen. From that we learned that free jumping sailfish were frequently traveling with friends, and if we got close enough to get out in front of them we might get a bite out of one or two of them. Another time we had four sailfish bite that way.

We got very intrigued with it and today any fisherman worth his salt, if he sees a free jumping sailfish, he does everything within his power to get in front of it and get as many baits out as he can. The guys up in the tuna towers can see all these sailfish swimming in the water and they'll tell their crew to throw a bait off the left side or the right side, or long cast left and so forth, whatever it takes to get a bait in front of these fish. In a tournament, where they're allowed to have four lines, they'll hook four sailfish and catch them. If they're allowed to have six lines they might catch six sailfish.

Free jumping sailfish, and any other jumping billfish, are a prime sign that you're in a position, if you're close enough, to present baits to a whole school of fish and really change your day in short order. And today we apply the same thing when we see jumping dolphin. We know we've got to get in front of them. If you see a free jumping swordfish, most of the time when he gets done jumping, he might be tailing and you might get a bite out of him too. If you see a free jumping billfish, get over there and get a bait in the water. It might pay big dividends.

Marty Klickenberg's Tarpon

At one time I had really gotten the tarpon off Bal Harbor wired. We had figured how to consistently catch these fish. We had gone from fishing with live mullet and switched over to use a lot of live shrimp, and boy, the tarpon there just loved that. The tarpon fishery was still in its heyday then. It hadn't been damaged by commercial netting yet.

I called up the writer for the Miami News, Marty Klinkenberg, and invited him to go tarpon fishing for the day. So Marty and I went out on my dad's boat, the *Moon Track*, a twenty-seven foot single diesel aluminum boat that my brother and dad built together. We went out off Bal Harbor to fish for these tarpon. It was a beautiful calm day, and the tarpon were loving it. We were going to have an article for the newspaper like never before. We had Marty's first big tarpon. Marty was fighting a big tarpon in the bow and I was fighting a tarpon in the back of the boat. I would beat my tarpon to where it was floating on the surface fifty to seventy-feet behind the boat. Because Marty was hooked up in the bow, I didn't want to disadvantage him, so I wouldn't back down on my fish. I would just wind on him hoping to quickly bring him alongside and turn him loose. But each time I pulled him forward the tarpon would revive again and I would have to fight it again.

Then it would float again and I would try to pull it to the boat and that would revive it again. This happened three or four times before I finally told Marty I had to back up and get that fish.

After I released my fish I grabbed my thirty-five millimeter camera and took pictures of Marty catching one tarpon after another. And I was bragging about my shots. "Oh, I got that one jumping over your head." Or, "I got that one full frame with the hotels in the background." And, "Oh, I got that one jumping off the transom of the boat." I was bragging about my pictures left and right, and Marty was having the time of his life, one tarpon after another on twenty-pound spinning tackle. It was really a banner day.

How many did he catch? I can't remember, maybe a half dozen or more. I know I caught a couple myself. But my pictures were going to be impeccable. This was going to be the newspaper article of the year.

At the end of fishing we went back to the dock. When we got off the boat Marty suggested I give him my roll of film. He was going to get it processed at the paper, and we would be good to go. I opened up the camera, and there was no film. Marty and I had to go out another day to get pictures of jumping tarpon for the article. What an embarrassment. All this bragging about these shots and there was no film in the camera. Oh well, such is life.

Moby Dick

Phil Conklin was my mate on this trip when I was chartering out of the Castaways Motel. We had an afternoon convention trip on the *Good Time IV*. Busses would pull up and unload untold numbers of guys. We would put six on each boat. These guys were all from big corporations that were having conventions in town. As a part of their treat for the week they would have their choice of fishing, golf, or tennis. So these were the guys who chose fishing.

Frequently they were just coming out of their business meetings. We would have box lunches and water and soft drinks on board for them. On our way out of the marina my mate would ask them if they wanted to buy some beer. If they said they did, Phil would collect the money for the beer and I would back up to this little marine store. Phil would run in, get the beer, run back out, jump aboard, and off we'd go fishing. Every once in a while some of these guys would have found time for a several martini lunch before getting on the boat.

This one trip it was blowing about fifteen out of the east, so there was a bit of a sea building. We went straight out the inlet and started trolling in about three or four hundred feet of water. We found a tree branch floating in the water, and by the branch we caught seven or eight nice eight to ten pound dolphins, nice fish. They showed a lot of color and our guys had a lot of fun catching them, then we'd put them in the fish box.

This guy who had a little bit to drink hollered, "These fish ain't big enough. I need Moby Dick." He continued ranting and using expletives about how he was going to catch Moby Dick's butt, and what he was going to do with him. Moby Dick this, and Moby Dick that, standing in the cockpit yelling out over the ocean. Moby Dick was this and Moby Dick so and so.

At this point in my career I had never seen a whale. And very shortly after this guy started hollering, lo and behold, east of me is a southbound whale. It was bigger than the boat, and I was awestruck. The people down in the cockpit couldn't see the whale, and I had to turn to not run into it. I turned southwest and hollered down to the drunk, "Hey you, noisy one. There's a guy out here looking for you."

He looked out and there was Moby Dick. He started yelling again about how he was going to whip Moby Dick, and beat Moby Dick, and this thing and that. Well, Moby Dick changed course and instead of heading straight south, he headed southwest which would converge with my course. So I turned southwest because I didn't want to get any closer to the whale. We ended up with the whale 200 feet behind the boat. And we had baits 100 feet back. And don't you know that in front of the whale we were hooking and landing dolphin. But I didn't want to slow down because I didn't want the whale to catch up with the boat.

Now here was this drunk, down on his knees with his elbows on the fish box across the back of the boat pleading and crying, "Oh please Moby don't come and get me; I really didn't mean it. Oh, Moby, please don't sink the boat. Don't eat me. Please forgive me, I didn't mean a word I said." Everybody on the boat was just cracking up. But it really did cause concern when that whale sunk out of sight and I didn't know where he was going. I knew nothing about whales in the ocean and how they would respond to the boat.

There were some tense moments until I finally decided he had left the area. Talk about timing, to have a guy cussing Moby Dick, and there's the first whale I've ever seen. And I'll tell you what, in all my career, maybe at the most I've seen ten whales off South Florida and it's a treat every time. What a thrill to see these massive animals.

The Draws of Bimini

People ask me all the time, "What draws you to Bimini in the Bahamas for a charter?" There are a number of different things. The first thing I think of about going to Bimini is the numerous shallow water wrecks. The east side of Bimini for twenty miles to the north and a hundred miles to the south is all water less than thirty feet deep. Especially during the marijuana smuggling times a lot of airplanes crashed within twenty miles of Bimini. On top of that over the years, boats have sunk, caught fire and sunk, or gone down for numerous reasons within twenty or thirty miles of Bimini. So in this shallow water there are a lot of artificial reefs or wrecks that draw an abundance of fish. It's an amazing thing to be in twenty-five feet of water with nothing but sand and grass for miles and miles on the ocean floor, and find an oasis where I can anchor up the boat and the cobia come running up to greet us and the barracudas are already swimming all over the top. We put out a chum bag and the water turns yellow with yellowtail snappers. There are mangrove snappers and small and large sharks wandering in the background looking to pick off a bait or injured fish. There's everything you could imagine, African pompano, permit, giant kingfish, cero mackerel, ballyhoo, and the list just goes on and on. We might pull up to a wreck and catch nothing but barracudas. But if we catch one of those we can hang it dead off the side of the boat we can catch sharks. We throw live bait, or plugs, or flies and catch sharks from ten to a hundred pounds. They run and jump and fight like the best game fish in the world.

We can ply the bottom with live bait and catch a plethora of assorted different kinds of snappers, even half-breed snappers where a yellowtail has mated with a lane snapper, or a mangrove snapper, any number of different combinations. And how good does it get? Dixie Burns caught three yellowtails on a plug with three treble hooks on one cast. A couple of times we caught two groupers on the same plug at the same time. We've caught giant world record cero mackerel, world record kingfish, numerous world record horse eyed jacks. The list goes on and on of phenomenal catches on these shallow wrecks way up on the bank.

Some of the fish are huge. We have gone on wrecks and chummed up yellowtails; and the yellowtails have attracted the amberjacks. We've caught fifty and sixty pound amberjacks on fly. You just can't imagine what these oases in the sea can provide. That's our first choice of things that happen when we go to Bimini.

We run a thirty-three foot, twin engine, center console Dusky. Bimini is the only place we go where we can consistently go fishing for bonefish in a boat this size. In the residential canals there are schools of bonefish. We drive up there with Abie in the bow with an angler. They signal for me to stop the boat, and they cast a small piece of conch or a small jig into a school of 250 bonefish. They catch bonefish cast after case from a thirty-three foot center console boat. It's a thrill to add a few bonefish to your day's catch. We do that regularly. On top of that there are any number of beaches in Bimini where you can wade in and catch bonefish, pompanette, which is a beautiful small cousin of a permit, snook, barracudas, or small sharks. The list goes on and on when it comes to wading ankle deep in the surf with a light spinning rod and a bucktail. It's amazing the number of things you can do in Bimini with shallow water fishing.

Then there's always the beach parties. When we go with the Dusky group we go to Honeymoon Harbor or Skull Beach, or some remote sandy beach where there's pure white sand. We chum up the stingrays and everybody is hand feeding them and petting them. There are also some pretty wild cocktail combinations. Things got really crazy one day when all of the rum punch and tequila punch were gone. Kevin Cote got a three-gallon bucket that I swear had been used for ground chum earlier. They poured a bottle of rum in it and collected mixers from different boats. They were passing around this three-gallon bucket and everybody in the crowd, men and women both, were drinking out of the plastic three-gallon Starbright bucket. It was really crazy.

I got lucky one day. I was designated as the Uber for all the women in the crowd. So I ran back the seven miles from Honeymoon Harbor to South Bimini with about a dozen beautiful women of all ages on my boat. We pulled into the Bimini Sands Harbor and all the girls were up on the bow dancing to the calypso music as we went round and round the harbor letting everybody eat their hearts out. It's just a wonderful place.

And then there's the general diversity of fishing, anchoring in fifty-five feet of water having hundreds of yellowtails behind the boat and the potential for fifty-pound groupers and snappers coming up off the bottom. We send out a live yellowtail, and a fifty or sixty pound kingfish might eat it. Or put out a small yellowtail and catch a ten pound cero

142

mackerel or a twenty-pound horse eyed jack. The potential is limitless, and it is so much fun.

Also there's the blue water where we can troll all day for dolphin or blue marlin, white marlin, wahoo, all different kinds of tunas, the list is limitless. And running back and forth to Bimini, whether going over or coming back, there's the potential for spotting whales. Our last trip home we spotted a whole pod of sperm whales including a cow with a calf. It was a sight my sister, Sue, Abie and his wife, Yudith, and I will never forget.

What a great place to go for a fun few days of boating and fishing.

How We Discovered Pat Brown's Fish Salad

We had just come across from Miami and we all gathered at Pat and Ralph Brown's condo at Bimini Sands. Abie Raymond was there, Mike Moon, Ralph, Pat, and Mike Brown, and me. We were sitting around talking about going to the restaurant when Mrs. Brown opened up the refrigerator and asked if anybody needed an appetizer. Abie and Mike Moon both chimed in that they were about to starve to death. So Mrs. Brown pulled out some crackers and a bowl of fish salad. Abie Raymond and Mike Moon wiped out the whole bowl. It was probably a quart of fish salad, and by the time they were done it was gone and they were ready to go to the restaurant for dinner. I don't know where they were going to squeeze it in.

But I asked Mrs. Brown about her recipe and she generously shared it with me: In a large saucepan pour a thin layer of white wine. Finely dice onions and celery, add them to the saucepan, and sweat the vegetables. When the vegetables have gotten tender, add two cups of water and a generous amount of salt. Or for different flavors, you can use chicken stock, vegetable stock, or beef stock. To this add largely cubed chunks of raw tuna, wahoo, or kingfish. Almost any fish will work, but oily fish are best. Bring this to a boil. When it begins to boil, be sure to skim off any proteins that come to the surface. In approximately five minutes pull out a large chunk of fish. If it cuts easily or separates easily with a fork, all your cooking is done, so you can remove the saucepan from the heat. Again scrape any remaining proteins off the surface and then strain the meat and vegetables into a strainer and allow it to cool. Break up the fish into fine pieces with your hands. Add mayonnaise and stir vigorously. At this point you can add capers or finely diced peppers to taste. Chill and serve with crackers, or for that matter on a sandwich. This is a great way to use tuna, wahoo, and kingfish – it makes a great cold salad.

As a sidebar, on occasions where you have leftover tuna, wahoo, or kingfish, or any other fish for that matter, you can sweat the vegetables, add the fish, no water necessary, and no heating required, break up the fish into fine particles, add the vegetables, again capers and peppers to your taste, add mayonnaise, stir thoroughly and serve with crackers, or as we said before in a sandwich. This is Pat Brown's seafood salad.

Islamorada Best

In the mid 1970s Tommy Ribel, Ubbie Adams, and Tommy Whitmore introduced B.J. and me to fishing the bridges in Islamorada. It was really a hoot. We would stop in Homestead, buy a bunch of live shrimp, put them in a cooler with an aerator, and then drive down to Indian Key Bridge. We would unload the car right on the bridge in between traffic pauses, and fish off the bridge all night and into the next day. And boy, what fun it was. When the traffic slowed down we would walk down toward the west end of the bridge away from the catwalk and throw mirror lures across the grass flat. Retrieving the lures across the flat we would catch big mangrove snappers, snook, and tarpon all night long. Just phenomenal action. As long as there was an outgoing tide going across that flat we were in business.

When the sun would come up in the morning we would fish on the downstream side of the bridge on the catwalk and catch cero and Spanish mackerel as our primary game. I remember one day I jigged up some moonfish, or lookdowns, and the goliath groupers (back then we called them Jewfish) would come along and eat my lookdowns and put on a really exciting time as these giant blobs would come up off the bottom and show themselves.

One morning I looked at the shrimp bucket and there were two little bitty shrimp. So I put on a number eight gold hook and hooked a shrimp through the head. Then I tied it to my twelve-pound test. I was thinking I might catch a mackerel, or blue runner, or jack or something, and lo and behold, I hooked a tarpon well over one hundred pounds. He jumped off into the sunrise and quickly ate through my line. So I tied on another little gold hook, hooked on the little bitty shrimp, and floated it out with the tide again, thinking mackerel, blue runner, jack, or a lookdown. Lo and behold, there was another tarpon over one hundred pounds, jumping off into the distance. It was a really exciting time even though the fish weren't caught. It was still a great time that exemplifies how much tarpon are attracted to really small baitfish. A lot of times you can catch big tarpon with small baits as opposed to big baits.

We would go to the tackle shops down there, and these guides would come in looking deeply dark tanned with white around their eyes from their sunglasses. There was nothing I wanted more than to be an Islamorada flats guide. They would come in with tales of tarpon and bonefish and permit, snook and redfish, and I would just stand there mesmerized visualizing all the great fishing they did.

When I graduated from high school I knew that in my future there would be a job as an Islamorada flats guide. I waited several years to save up the money to make the move to go into business for myself. Over time I arranged to buy Jim Brewer's flats skiff. Jim was a famous flats guide. He lost his life in an airplane scouting tarpon for a tournament. I bought his boat from his widow thanks to help from Jesse Webb from Pflueger Taxidermy. Jesse also got me hooked up to where I could run out of Bud and Mary's Marina. So I had it made. I told my boss, Lou Filetta, that I would be leaving *Doctor's Orders* on March 1, 1976 to be a flats guide in the Keys. I gave him plenty of notice, and off I went with my bonefish skiff behind my white pickup truck and headed for the Keys.

Thanks to a young lady who worked for the Ft. Lauderdale News, I had arranged to rent a small cottage on the side of a house in Lower Matecumbe. I could walk out every morning and watch the bonefish tailing on the grass flats right behind the apartment. It was a short drive up to Bud and Mary's where I would be leave to go fishing with live mullet around the bridges. We would either catch the live mullet, or more often than not, Frank the Net would pull into the parking lot and sell live mullet to any boat that was going live bait tarpon fishing. Then we would run down to Channel Two or Channel Five and fish for tarpon. While tarpon fishing we would occasionally catch a snook, and we caught a lot of barracudas, or an occasional jack crevalle. During the latter part of the season we switched over to crabs and pinfish, and we could pick up a permit or two doing that.

Another thing we did a lot of was bone fishing. We would either pole the flats on the ocean side or on the bayside, or we would stake up and chum with shrimp and wait for the bonefish to come to us. We could sight cast, or just cast baits out, and let the baits sit on the bottom until the bonefish came along and picked them up.

Our third option, which we did quite a bit because it provides a lot of action, was running back to Flamingo and catching sea trout and snook and an occasional redfish, tarpon, or shark. We would go to Springer Bank where we would catch loads of Spanish mackerel, some sea trout, and mangrove snappers. Whatever it was, we were always having fun. Just for spice, every once in a while we would take a bucket of live shrimp and go out and fish the patch reefs for hog fish, porgies, and mutton snappers. We would get some permit from time to time doing that. It was such a diversity of fishing. I was living my dream fishing out of Bud and Mary's, getting that dark tan and the white rings around my eyes; that famous raccoon eyes as a flats guide. What a treat it was.

I met some great people when I was down there. Sonny Fisher was the marina manager. He was a really nice guy from the Delmarva Peninsula. He lived in Maryland on the east side of Chesapeake Bay. Vic Gaspenny and Theresa Huckins had come down from the Carolinas and I made great friends with them and John Kipp.

The number one guy from my life down there was Sonny Eslinger. One season I shared a trailer with Sonny after my first summer. After my first season on Lower Matecumbe we went to Ocean City Maryland for the summer. When I came back I shared a trailer with Sonny and we were sailing out of Bud and Mary's everyday. Then Jack Plactor and Craig Koch came down the following season and I shared a trailer with them. Jack and Craig were running a charter boat and that afforded me an option to go offshore once in a while too.

Boy, what a great time it was fishing down there all through the winter and spring up until about the end of June. Then we would go to Ocean City, Maryland for the summer and fish for white marlin. We'd return to the Keys about the first of November and spend the winters there. But it was great memories of great times with Sonny Eslinger. That gang was a bunch of great people. It was a really wonderful stage in my life.

This adventure as a Florida Keys guide was only possible due to my wonderful wife Ruth. She worked at North Miami General Hospital. Her dependable job and understanding of my obsessions with fishing made my dreams come true. When she got sick, I had to settle down with a steady job close to home. This return to Miami fishing was the start of my good fortunes with my fishing business in Miami.

Butter Snapper

I was running charters out of Bahia Mar in Ft. Lauderdale in 1975 and 1976. My charter boat being new at the dock was all the way to the south end of the charter dock. It was a forty-seven foot Pacemaker called *Doctor's Orders*. Behind every boat was an open-air fish market. We all had rolls of wrapping paper, scales, and nice clean cutting tables. We would lay down wrapping paper and ice and then put a sheet of wrapping paper over them. The people would drive in at the north end of the dock as far away from me as they could get. They would stop at the different boats asking what kind of fish they had.

As has always gone on in the fishing industry, a lot of the fish had local names. In Ft. Lauderdale amberjack was called butter snapper. Snapper always sold well, so everybody called them butter snapper. I never felt right about calling amberjacks snappers so, being at the low end of the totem pole, I had to do something new, so I just called mine amberjacks.

I was up at the north end of the dock one day and a car pulled in with two women in it and they stopped at the first boat. They called out, "What kind of fish you got in there boys?"

"We've got some beautiful butter snapper."

She pulled up to the next boat, "What have you got?"

150

"Sorry, all I've got is butter snapper."

She drove on two more boats down and called out, "What have you got?"

"I've got butter snapper and kingfish."

She continued down the dock and by then I recognized her. I had sold her fish a few days earlier. While she was stopping and checking and calling out only to find the boats had butter snapper, or kingfish, or some didn't have anything, I hurried on down to our boat. When she got down to me I told her the same thing I told her last time. I had some beautiful amberjack. She said, "OK, give me a whole bunch of it." It was a nice purchase of five or six pounds of amberjack filet.

She went on her way thrilled to death. I had to chuckle because all these other guys were selling the same fish by a phony name. She hadn't had butter snapper, but she knew she liked amberjack, and I had amberjack to fill the bill. So all those guys missed out on the sale and I got the sale at the long end of the dock.

That was the fish market at Bahia Mar. And just a little sidebar, when things were really slow I would catch blowfish off the back of the boat right there at the end of the dock and called them blowfish, also known as sea squab.

Mark Sosin

I have a lot of writer friends who are more or less my same age or even younger in some cases. Before any of us really got off and running, Mark Sosin was leading the charge in salt water fishing and writing, and then in TV. Then he joined George Poveromo on the stage and truly was the pioneer in public media on fishing. And because he was several years ahead of us, he was definitely my idol as I was coming up in the game.

Mark and I got off on a really rough start. He gave a presentation at the Miami Beach Rod and Reel Club, and I was awestruck because here was my hero. I was really proud of myself because I had established a great tarpon fishery off Bal Harbor. I went up to Mark after his presentation as he was surrounded by other admirers. I told him I had a charter boat business for tarpon fishing off the north end of Miami Beach, and it would be an honor if he would like to join me for a TV show or write an article, either one. Mark's answer was, "Son, I wouldn't use you on TV or in an article on a bet."

Well, I turned away and thought to myself, 'The hell with you,' and went on about making a career for myself. As luck would have it, about a year later I received a phone call and, lo and behold, it was Mark Sosin.

Mark said, "Captain Bouncer, I'm in a bind, and several people have told me that you're the man to save me." It seems that Mark had contracted with the State to make a video on how to release fish with the best chance of the fish surviving. This included six days of fishing, and he had already fished for seven days and had one release. He needed to catch more fish and let them go.

I told him I thought I could fill the bill for him and that we could go any day in the upcoming week. So we set a date and headed out on my Dusky 256. We netted pilchards somewhere around Haulover Inlet, then we went out and anchored on the Spring Hole, which is in 130 feet of water right off the inlet. We started fishing pilchards on flat lines and on the bottom. To make a very long story short, in just a couple of hours we had seven species of fish and about ten different ways to release them. We had kingfish, and yellowtails, and muttons, just a plethora of stuff.

Mark was using union cameramen at the time and he said, "OK guys, it's just about twelve o'clock, let's break for lunch."

Mark and I kept fishing in the back of the boat and we hooked a good kingfish and I said, "Mark, don't you want to get the cameras rolling?"

He said, "No, the guys are on their lunch break." And don't you know it, right next to the boat a big bull shark came up and ate that kingfish. He put on a fantastic show and there were no cameras rolling. He explained to me later that when you use union cameramen, if you interrupted their lunch break, it was very expensive, and that's why he didn't have them rolling.

The bottom line was we had a very successful day. He went from zero for seven days, to get the video he needed in a half a day fishing off Haulover Inlet on my little old Dusky, and I was thrilled. Mark was thrilled as well and from it came a longtime wonderful friendship. OMG we did so many shows together. We did shows where we did a whole twenty-two minutes of good fishing TV in less than a day. But conversely we had one series where we spent eighteen days trying to make a show. Everything came together to thwart our efforts and we really struggled to finally complete that project.

In another really crazy Mark Sosin episode, we were fishing live shrimp for tarpon in Government Cut. So Mark and one cameraman and I were on Mark's boat, and we were using my Dusky as the camera boat. Mark hooked a really good fish and it started to run across the channel. Usually on the first run a tarpon will come up and jump, so I said to Mark, "He's headed for the tip of the north jetty." I said this out loud so the cameraman who was hearing everything we said would know where to aim the camera. Lo and behold, it ran along the tip of the north jetty, but it didn't jump. Then it went back deep in the channel and Mark was fighting it, and it took off for the tip of the south jetty.

Mark hollered, "There it goes toward the tip of the south jetty, maybe it will jump this time." But sure enough it didn't jump. It kept going back and forth, and back and forth, but it never came up and jumped. After a really great battle, up came this beautiful forty-pound permit, and then we knew why it didn't do much jumping. But what a great catch!

Then there was the time we were live baiting on the kite. Mark had been through all of our style of hooking bait on circle hooks on the kite, and he knew that when a fish ate the bait on the kite to wait for the fish to pull the line out of the clip, and then wind tight and get the fish. So here came this big yellowfin tuna, jumping into the air and grabbed our kite bait and dove into the depths. Nobody was going to yell at Mark, "wind, wind, wind," which would be the correct thing to do.

You've got to come tight on a tuna really quick. Mark waited for the line to come tight, and unfortunately by then the tuna had spit out the bait. But what a beautiful strike. Something that I'll always remember about that is Mark following directions to a tee but losing this fish. He did it the way we told him, so we couldn't knock that.

One of the most amazing days was with Abie Raymond. We were permit fishing down off the Doc Demille. Mark had caught five or six permit already and then hooked another one. Now here's a guy who is in his early seventies and he said. "Abie, I need you to take the rod for a few minutes." Abie fought the permit for a while and when it got close to the boat Mark decided to take it back and finish the catch.

We added it to the TV show and at one point right when it happened Abie said, "So this is how it's all done?" and was a little disenchanted. But when Abie saw how much drag he had used and how hard Mark had been fighting and, considering the fact that Mark was more than forty years older than Abie, Abie realized the respect he owed Mark for all the fish he had caught. And quite frankly, that was about the only time in fifteen or so shows that I ever saw Mark hand off the rod.

Mark and I also took fun fishing trips. I took his grandchildren on one of the most embarrassing days of my life. Here I had Mark Sosin and several of his grandkids, and I think one of his sons was with us. We were fishing in the bay but not catching anything, so I decided to go out Cape Florida and take them offshore. It was pretty rough coming out of the Cape, and here came this big wave. I had two choices, speed up and hit the wave, or slow down and slide over it. I slowed down, but the wave broke over the top of the bow. Now we had Mark's grandkids floating around in the cockpit of the boat, soaking wet and scared to death. I took them back into the bay and we saved the day by catching some nice groupers, and snappers, and blue runners. The kids had a ball, but it was the last day that I ever got to fish with Mark, and I don't think he ever fully forgave me for shocking his grandkids so badly.

Still to this day every once in a while I'll give Mark a call. My hero is a lot like me, just about run out of steam. He had back surgery that didn't go too well. He lost his confidence and his sense of balance. Today it seems he spends most of his time in the house. I thank God that I still get to go fishing everyday, but I'll never forget my days with Mark.

Dear Mark Sosin, I hope you're around for along time to enjoy your sons and your grandchildren, and I know that I'll always enjoy every memory of our times together.

Martini's Nurse Shark

Martini Arostegui can be a really dangerous guy to fish with, but I don't think it's his fault. I think we just get too excited when we're fishing with him, and it has been a few years since we've been in grave danger in his presence. We were over in Bimini trying to catch a small fry world record shark, and nurse sharks were eligible. Well, nurse sharks in Bimini can be found in very shallow water, and they're not the most aggressive long running fish in the ocean.

So we went to a small wreck and looked down on the bottom, and there were a couple of big nurse sharks. We dropped down a big bait and Martini sat down in the fighting chair. A nurse shark ate the big bait and Martini hooked it and fought it for a while and brought it up to the boat. His dad, Marty, was getting a platform ready, a sheet to where we could slide the shark onto it and hook the four corners onto the scale, weigh the shark, and then slide it back into the water.

While he was getting that ready, Ron Jon Cook and I grabbed the small gaff and opened the tuna door. We gaffed the nurse shark in the corner of the mouth. As it came into the boat, and the gaff handle, which was a foam rubber material, went up inside my short sleeve shirtsleeve. Then the shark started to roll. In rolling it wound up that gaff handle inside my shirt so tight that it was peeling the skin off the inside of my arm. The pain was excruciating. The skin wasn't being burned off, or cut off, it was being ripped off my bicep. Did it hurt! Ron Jon finally got the shark under control, and we got the gaff out of my sleeve. We weighed the shark, discovered it was a world record, and we sent it on its way. We bandaged up my arm and went back to fishing.

Later on the same day we were out on the reef catching a wide variety of fish including some big horse-eyed jacks using live yellowtails for bait. Martini had a big horse-eyed jack on and Ron Jon was in the act of getting ready to boat it. The line had an eight-ounce egg sinker above the swivel. The horse-eyed jack came off with the rod bent over to the max and full tension on the line. The eight ounce sinker, like a giant musket ball, came back and hit Ron Jon right in the shin. How it didn't break that leg I'll never understand.

He laughed it off and we kept on fishing, but I'll tell you what, my arm sure hurt and I don't know how his leg didn't hurt. We sure had some great times with Martini, but that day he was downright dangerous.

Keep Your Eyes Open

So Abie and I fire up the Dusky 33 with twin Evinrudes every morning. We're sitting in our slip, the engines are running, and the customers are on board. We're ready to pull out of the slip. Abie and I are ever vigilant. As we're pulling out of our slip there's some bait flipping, or there's some bait marking on the depth finder. It might be a good place to throw the cast net if we're going for Spanish mackerel and we want small pilchards for bait. So we make a mental note, there's some bait in the marina, and it might be there again tomorrow morning.

As we clear the breakwater and start to head out Government Cut, we go by a buoy and, as we thought, the outgoing tide is running strong. We're looking right and left, watching for pods of bait along the sides of the channel. We're watching for diving birds, flipping bait, jumping mullet, any number of different things. The depth finder is on, and if it's calm enough we're running along the edge of the channel, and I'm watching the depth finder for signs of tarpon in the ship channel or tarpon or snook when we're up close to the jetty. We're glancing side to side. Are there pelicans diving on the south side of the south jetty, or are they diving at the tip of the north jetty? It might be schools of mullet, pilchards, herring, sardines, glass minnows, any number of different kinds of bait fish that might tip us off to a source of bait or a pod of game fish, either one.

As we go on out, we're watching the rips looking for any signs of fish. It could be a school of big jack crevalles. If you watch close on a rip outside an inlet with a line of grass, you may find permit feeding in that grass. We're working our way out toward the Bent Range Marker, watching the depth finder the whole time because the herring may be in closer than the marker. We make it to the Bent Range Marker where we're going to try to catch some live bait and we don't just stop and fire out the rigs. As we slow down and maneuver around the marker, we're watching the depth finder. Are we seeing schools of bait, or is it empty water?   There's a school of bait half way to the bottom. We tell our customers to drop their sabiki rigs half way to the bottom, or hit the bottom and wind up two cranks, or hit the bottom and wind up four cranks. Do this before they start to work their lures, because the depth finder tells them how far down to drop to the bait. So we've successfully got some live bait in the live well, whether we bought it from Frank on the *Ashley*, or we caught it ourselves, or it's a combination of both.

Now we leave the Bent Range Marker in twenty feet of water and head offshore. What are we going to do today? What we see will have a lot to do with that. As we go by a lobster pot buoy, or the sewer outfall off Government Cut, we see that the current is pushing to the north, or it's pushing to the south, or we have no current. The water at 100 feet is green, then there's a beautiful color change and the water turns blue in 120 feet. That's a really good spot, dark blue against green, no current against the north current. This is liable to be the spot for dolphin, sailfish, kingfish, bonitos, blackfin tunas, wahoos – the list is endless.

Or we may not get that sharp edge. We may get a gentle blend. When we get that gentle blend it means the fish are going to be blended in, they're not going to be in a tight marching line. It means we're going to have to cover more depths to find the fish. Maybe on the southeast wind this morning we'll have to start in 200 feet and drift back in to 100 feet and see where we find the most fish instead of setting up the kites on that sharp edge in 120 feet and just fishing that sharp edge.

These are things we see on our way out. Maybe we will see that there's a lot of scattered sargasum seaweed, which is going to make fishing more challenging. We may want to run a little more south or north to get out of the scattered grass because it makes fishing more difficult as the grass catches on everything we put in the water.

Whoa, there's a frigate bird in hot pursuit of ballyhoo showering in ninety feet of water. The water is not even blue, but the ballyhoo are showering and the frigate birds are going crazy. We run over there and find a fifteen- pound mahi mahi chasing these ballyhoo. So we fire out a herring but he won't eat it. Then we fire out a pilchard, and he won't eat that either. So we hook on a fresh dead ballyhoo and skid it across the top, and that mahi is all over it. The tip involved here is that if you're seeing ballyhoo being showered, you need to get some ballyhoo because those fish are going to be really hard to catch on any other kind of bait.

We'll say the frigate bird didn't materialize, so we're moving out a little deeper. Lo and behold, we see a lot of birds flying around in 100 to 200 feet of water. That means that they're finding food. So we set up a drift to see what comes our way, whether it's something down on the bottom or mid level. Now we're marking a lot of streaky, jagged lines about half way to the bottom. Better put on a wire leader and fish a bait at mid depth, because those jagged lines down there on your depth finder are kingfish. Or it may be pods of bait, but they also could have kingfish, bonitos, sailfish, tunas, anything. Those pods of bait are about eighty feet down so we need to put our bait down there.

OK, so the water was green and there wasn't any current; it didn't look exciting. There weren't any birds, so we keep going offshore. Slowly the water gets beautiful blue and we're still headed offshore looking for any sign of a fish. Oh my goodness, look over there! It looks like a lobster ball. White Styrofoam does not usually attract much. But it looks like it's a lobster ball, so we better go check it out. On that lobster ball, lo and behold, there's about 100 feet of coiled up nylon rope covered with barnacles. That's as good a floater as you'll ever find. As we troll by, sure enough here comes a five-pound dolphin, and we catch two or three nice dolphin.

I guess that's all the dolphin here so we might as well leave. But wait a minute, let's put on a planer and a three and a half drone spoon, or make it easy and tie on a Rapala X rap, an X-30, put that on a vertical jigging rod with a fifty-pound fluorocarbon leader and braided line, and let's troll that planer or the plug back and forth past that floater three or four times. We might pick up a wahoo; we won't know if we don't try. You can try a vertical jig, and maybe get that wahoo, but trolling a diving plug, or that planer with the three and a half drone is a lot more dependable.

OK, we wore it out. We caught three dolphin, no luck with the wahoo, so we keep on going. Over there are about twenty birds wheeling and diving and moving very fast. Let's head over there. Abie, what do you think? Birds wheeling and diving, and moving very fast. His advice is to put out the small feathers because that's going to be skipjack or maybe blackfin tunas. Put those feathers way back and troll them really fast. Get ahead of the birds and troll back and forth in front of them. Whoa, sure enough, there's a nice fifteen-pound skipjack tuna that's going to make some great poke tonight.

We head on offshore and there it is, a line of seaweed. We get next to it on the east side, which is a nice sharp edge. The west side is kind of broken up. We troll down the weed line and rip, and look under the grass but see no baitfish or birds flying. After a couple of miles with no barracuda or dolphin, or anything, it's just dead. No bait, no birds, no big game fish, we've got to get out of here, this is not a viable weed line.

In another mile there's another weed line, so we get along side of it and there's a little wake running along the surface. Oh, it's a puffer fish. And there's another wake, and it's a school of flying fish taking off. Then under the grass is a bunch of baby blue runners and sargasum fish. Now we see birds flying down the weed line. This is a good, live weed line. This deserves a lot of effort. You're going to find dolphin, wahoo, barracudas, billfish, tunas, just about anything going down this weed line. This is the place you want to be.

The key to everything I have been talking about here is looking as you go fishing. You've always got to keep a sharp eye out. Do you see mackerel skyrocketing on ballyhoo on the reef? Is the reef gin clear near the end of the year where you can troll that thirty foot reef and can see where the end of the reef is so you know where to drive the boat? A black grouper on that reef wouldn't have any trouble seeing your ballyhoo or feather swimming overhead and come up and slam it. Or is the reef real dirty where you can't see it and the black grouper can't see the bait, so this isn't a good place to troll for grouper. Is there a good sharp edge to concentrate a lot of game fish in 100 or 200 feet of water?

Listen on the radio. Do they have a sharp edge in 120 feet five miles to the south of where you are? Is taking the time to run to a better location more productive than sitting in green water, with no current, no bait, and catching nothing. Or is everybody stuck with dirty water and slow current so that the plan has to change to bottom fishing on wrecks and deep reefs?

Keeping your eyes open is so important. A lobster float with a hank of rope can make your whole day. A shower of ballyhoo in the wrong place in fifty feet of water, and finding that big dolphin instead of finding him five miles offshore is the reward for watching what's going on. Showers of ballyhoo on the reef are telling you that you should fish in fifty feet of water, slow trolling ballyhoo, instead of kite fishing in 150 because the bait and the game fish are migrating in shallow.

Keep your eyes open the same when fishing in the inlet. If you're looking for snook in the inlet, and the birds are all diving on the north side of the jetty, and you're on the south side of the jetty, you had better smarten up and go try the other side of the jetty. The birds are diving because that's where the baits are.

You can even tell by a blue heron. A blue heron standing on the rocks watching this spot or that spot indicates the predator fish have been pushing bait fish up against his feet where he can feed. You may want to concentrate on that area; it can make your whole day. I hope these lessons on keeping your eyes open will make a better fishing trip everyday for you.

And a little sidebar with this, teach your kids, or your guests from Ohio, or wherever they're from, to help. Make it a game. If you're the first person to spot the frigate bird, you get

164

the first bite under the frigate bird. If you're the first person to spot the bamboo tree floating five miles offshore, then you get to catch the first fish on the bamboo tree. Keep everybody involved. You've got a lot of jobs, drive the boat, take off the weed, rig fresh baits, and do it all again. Let your guests do what they are capable of doing, keep their eyes open.

Good luck, catch fish, and thank Pat Mansell for bringing it all to your attention.

Arthur Smith KDW Tournament Radio Gag

It was the Arthur Smith Kingfish Dolphin Wahoo Tournament. Ralph Brown, who owned Dusky Marine, and Bill Applegate, who worked for Ralph, and Ron Wigner, who worked for Evinrude, and I were fishing it together. We had chosen to go way offshore in search of big dolphin. We were probably closer to Great Isaacs Lighthouse than we were to Palm Beach, and there was not a boat in sight in any direction.

All of a sudden over the VHF radio came, "Hey, that Dusky boat sure is ugly looking."

Ralph Brown, who owns Dusky, spun around looking for the boat that was calling over the radio but couldn't see anything. And Ron Wigner from Evinrude was baffled too. "Who the heck is calling us?"

The voice on the radio came back on and said, "Yeah, I see you guys looking around." Now the hair on the back of Ron Wigner's neck was all bristled up, and Ralph was trying to figure what the heck was going on.

About that time the voice on the radio came back on and said, "By the way, you better watch the cushion on the bow of the boat. It's about to go overboard." Ron and Ralph looked up there and sure enough, the cushion on the bow was a little bit out of place. It was not going anywhere any time soon, but it was definitely out of place. Ron and Ralph are totally dumbfounded as to who was talking.

There was about twenty minutes of silence and then, "Hey you guys on the Dusky, aren't you ever going to catch any fish? You guys gotta be the two ugliest guys I've ever seen, Ron Wigner and Ralph Brown. You guys is ugly!"
Now Ron and Ralph were really getting their dander up. They couldn't figure out what was going on and neither could I.

Bill Applegate was standing in the back of the boat standing like an Indian chief watching the baits. We were trolling along and I went back there, and caught in the crook of his arm, Bill had a hand held VHF radio, firing these guys up with these comments. And none of us realized we were being scammed.

But that's OK because I took care of Bill Applegate real well. I stayed back there in the back for a while then I moseyed up to the front and tipped the guys that Bill Applegate was the one who was making those comments. I think they used a saltwater wash down hose, but it might have been a bucket. Either way, the next time the radio went off with a smart Alec comment about the beautiful boat, Bill Applegate got doused with seawater and the gig was up.

It was sure fun while it was taking place. That was the good old days of the Arthur Smith Kingfish Dolphin Wahoo Tournaments.

Yancy Trying to Get the Baits Out

Yancy Perkins was my mate one year out of Miami Beach Marina. He only worked my tarpon trips out at night. We had a system down that worked really well. We would bait all the rods, and then I would stop the boat and explain to the customers what was going to happen. Yancy was going to throw their bait in the water and hand them the rod with the bail open. They would let their line run out until I told them to close the bail. We would go in a big semi circle and Yancy would fire out the first bait and the angler would take it up to the bow. Then he'd fire out the second bait and that angler would put it in the middle of the boat. Then Yancy would fire out the third bait and Yancy would put it in the back of the boat. In no time at all we would go from being stopped, to going in a semi circle and having all the baits out far enough to fish and ready to make our drift. We just made a semi-circle, drift downwind running out all the lines as I made the turn, and everything would be in position when I stopped the boat to let us drift.

One day I wasn't going night fishing so Matty Tambor asked Yancy to go with him. So Yancy jumped on Matty's boat and asked, "Where are the circle hooks?"

Matty said, "Oh, no. We're not using circle hooks for tarpon. We want to use these little j-hooks." So Yancy tied the j-hooks on with a loop knot and Matty said, "No, they have to be snelled." So Yancy snelled the hooks on after Matty showed him how. They went out and stopped in the tarpon's hole, and by then Yancy had all the hooks baited. Matty stopped the boat and Yancy said, "OK, we're ready to put them out."

Matty said, "OK, go ahead."

And Yancy said, "Go forward with the boat."

Matty said, "What are you talking about? Just let the lines out."

So Yancy put the lines out telling Matty that the baits were going to sink to the bottom and get eaten by the grunts. But Matty said, "No, this is the way we do it. Just hand line the lines out and we'll be good to go."

They went fishing for several hours, and every time Yancy hand lined the lines out the little fish on the bottom would chew their shrimp off, and they would either catch the little critters or come in with no bait.

The next night I was off again and another good friend of mine, Doug Coven, asked Yancy to go with him. So Yancy said, "Oh yeah. I'd love to go with you. I love my tarpon fishing." He asked, "What hooks do you want to use?"

Doug said, "Use these circle hooks." So Yancy tied loop knots on the circle hooks and Doug said, "Oh no. They have to be improved clinch knots. They have to be cinched down tight."

So Yancy tied them all with improved clinch knots and they went out the inlet and baited all the hooks. They got out to where they were going to fish and Doug stopped the boat. Yancy said, "OK, the rods are baited. We're ready to run them out."

169

Doug said, "What are you talking about?"

Yancy said, "Yeah, you start going forward and I'll put one in the water and let it run out, then circle around and we'll do the second one, and then the third one."

Doug said, "What, are you crazy? Just hand line them out and lock them up and we'll be all set to go."

Once again Yancy hand lined the baits out, locked them up. Ultimately he wound them up with bare hooks at the end of the drift. That went on for two or three hours with no bites, no fish, no bait, and Yancy was tearing his hair out. I can't begin to tell you how happy he was to be back out fishing with me again the next night.

So, once again, if you're not sure how we did it, we would bait all three rods. And we'd have all three lines hanging in the boat either in the live well or in a bucket of water. I would start a semi circle downwind. As soon as I went forward with the boat I would call out, "Fire one," and Yancy would fire out the first bait, give the rod to the customer with the bail open. That angler would walk up to the bow on the downwind side of the boat. Then as I turned downwind, the second line would be ready to go, and Yancy would throw that one overboard. He'd hand the rod to the second angler and tell him to let the line run out with the bail open and to stop in the middle of the boat. Then Yancy would start the third bait, and by the time I had completed a semi circle, having started to the south and now half way around and pointed north, all three lines would be out 100 or 150 feet, depending on how much line I wanted out. One guy would be in the bow with his bail closed ready to fish. One guy would be in the middle of the boat with his bail closed ready to fish, and one guy would be in the back with the bail closed ready to fish. They would be spread out from seventy-five to one hundred twenty-five feet, or fifty to one hundred feet, depending on how much wind was blowing was how big a semi circle I made. By the time I stopped going forward with the boat, all the lines were stretched out and the baits were up near the surface. The wind would start to carry us downwind and we would have no problem with the baits sinking down to the bottom.

We had it down to a science. It worked really great. If you ever want to give it a try, give me a call and I'll talk you through it. What a great way to put those baits out, whether you are drifting for sailfish with live pilchards, or drifting with live shrimp for tarpon, both times the system works really well.

It's Time to Go

Yancy Perkins was my night mate and an avid fly fisherman. I introduced him to tarpon fishing, and he could not get enough action. He became a tarpon fishing addict. When we went out he always brought a fly rod with him, and when we were drifting with live shrimp or crabs, he'd be flipping a fly looking for tarpon. If he got lucky enough to hook one, he'd hand it off to the customers.

I kept telling him about when the shrimp ran at night it would be like casting to rising trout in a Wyoming river where he was from. One night we were out there and it was getting time to go home, and all of a sudden here come the shrimp and the tarpon. The tarpon were blasting all around the boat and we'd hook a tarpon on shrimp as fast as we could throw the baits out. We settled down and released our second tarpon really quick. The tarpon were blowing up all around the boat, but it was now past time to go home.

I said, "Yancy, this is what you've been waiting all year for, wind em up, it's time to go home."

It broke his heart. He bought a boat and motor within two weeks. So when I told him it was time to go home, he'd be able to jump on his own boat and get back out there. He became so addicted on this nighttime fly-fishing for tarpon that he actually slept on his boat all night out where the tarpon and shrimp usually showed up. He would be woken up by the sound of tarpon busting shrimp, and he would be fly casting at three, four, five o'clock in the morning.

You should have seen his face when I said, "Yancy, that's how good it can get. It's time to go home."

Grandpa's Color of the Water

My grandfather, Ernest Beach Smith, was a world-renowned artist. He started off in Detroit doing commercial art, and ended up as a Southwest United States artist who did a big mural in the capitol in Arizona. He was one of the first artists in the artists' retreat that Jerome, Arizona, became later on. He moved to Florida in his mid seventies, and by then he had done paintings for each of his grandchildren as they graduated from high school. My sister got a painting of herself with a few of the black eyed Susans, and other grandkids got other paintings.

But my painting came as a composite. I had caught a sailfish when I was eight years old, and I stood next to it on the dock with no shirt on. He captured me as a little boy with no shirt on. I gave my grandfather a picture of my mounted sailfish on the wall, so my sailfish was jumping out of the water in the painting. I sent him a picture of me holding a fishing rod with a red pennant that indicated a sailfish release when I was in my early teens, and that became a part of the picture as well. So here was this beautiful composite picture of a sailfish jumping out of the ocean, me holding a rod with a release flag, and a little boy with no shirt on. But the water was almost a split pea soup green. That was the only thing that was kind of out of place on it.

When Grandpa moved to Florida I was working on a head boat, and I took him out for a ride. It was a beautiful summer day, and it was nice and calm. We were going through the green water, and Grandpa was thrilled to be there to see the ocean like this. He had never seen the Atlantic Ocean before. Then we came to a beautiful, spectacular blue green color change where the inshore waters met the roaring currents of the Gulf Stream. It was a line of demarcation just as sharp as black and white would be. This was peas soup green changing to deep deep blue.

I said to Grandpa, "This deep blue water is where we find sailfish." And with that, my very old grandfather who was ill and unstable, began to cry. I asked, "Grandpa, what's the matter?"

Grandpa said to me, "When I did your painting, I painted your sailfish jumping out of beautiful blue water, and I thought to myself, 'No water could be so blue.' So I completely redid all the water in your painting in that green color because I didn't think water could be so blue. And now I see I should have left it blue, and I'm really disappointed that I let you down."

I said, "Grandpa, you could never let me down. You've been an inspiration in my life. And thank you for a great painting."

Stabbed by a Sailfish

Benji Hiller was a client I mentioned in other stories. He had an adopted son, Daniel, and a natural born son, Gabriel. It was one of our earlier trips and Benji and Daniel were down here fishing with me. It was during the Mini Met and we were targeting sailfish. We were fishing off the south end of Miami Beach.

At around noon we finally hooked a sailfish. Daniel had it on and it put up a good fight. As we fought it I noticed that it had gotten the line wrapped around its tail. When a sailfish is tail wrapped the fish goes until it is totally exhausted. We were going to have to pull this fish in backwards. Now we have gotten pretty good at reviving them, but back then it was pretty much touch and go whether we would get them up in time before they were totally dead. As quickly as I could I brought us up close to it and got hold of the leader. While pulling the fish in the leader broke. I turned to Daniel and congratulated him on his first sailfish.

Daniel said, "Oh thank you. That was so much fun. How could you tell it was tail wrapped?"

I said, "Well, first of all it's a slow steady jerk on the rod. Every time the fish swishes its tail it jerks on the rod. Then when the fish is relatively close you can see the line runs to the base of the tail as opposed to the mouth. The fish stops jumping because it is being pulled backwards."

Not much more than ten minutes later we hooked another sailfish and Benji took the rod. This was his first also, so he was fighting this sailfish, and Daniel was also in the back of the boat taking pictures as the fish jumped. We got the fish up to the boat and I grabbed it by the bill and lifted it half way out of the water. Benji leaned over and we got some pictures and released it.

Daniel asked, "How come you didn't take pictures of my fish like that?" I reminded him that his fish was tail wrapped and we could not get control of it before the leader broke.

I said, "But don't worry, the way they're biting now you'll probably catch another one." So we put the baits out again and sure enough, in very short order we hooked another sailfish. So Daniel fought this one, and it was running and jumping and putting on a great show. We were having a ball, but Benji was repeatedly telling us how the pictures would never come out because he was the world's worst photographer. (And we did verify that Benji was indeed the world's worst photographer.)

At any rate, Daniel was fighting the fish and Benji was trying to get pictures while I was driving the boat. We finally got the fish close to boat and I grabbed the leader and the fish raced toward the bow and came up and jumped. (It was a perfect opportunity for Benji to get a picture, but I'm sure he didn't get anything but maybe a splash.) I was pulling on the leader when the fish jumped, and it raced right back toward the outboard motors and did another beautiful jump. I pulled it off balance when it jumped and it came right back toward Daniel. It came right alongside of the boat and jumped. It was putting on a beautiful show. Well, this time when it hit the water it was

176

headed back toward the boat and headed right toward Daniel. Daniel was standing at the edge of my helm seat/back seat combo, and was backed up against the seat and had no place to go left or right.

I saw that this sailfish was coming in the boat, so I pushed Daniel back toward the motors, and in doing that I ended up where he had been standing. I turned just as the sailfish came over the side of the boat and he hit me just above the belt with his bill. I pushed the fish back overboard and I was afraid to look to see what condition I was in. I've heard stories of people getting seriously injured this way.

But boy, was I lucky! The sailfish's bill was broken off and healed over, so instead of being as sharp as a relatively sharpened pencil, it was about as sharp as the end of my index finger. It had been rounded off. Also, it was probably six or eight inches shorter than normal. Under normal conditions in what had happened, the bill of the sailfish would have gone half way through my body. But the bill, being dull, and being shorter, I was lucky to have a heck of a black bruise on my belly and just the slightest trickle of blood, instead of a disastrous situation. The sailfish actually stayed on and we got him up and got pictures of him before we sent him on his way. Boy was I lucky.

Just as a little sidebar, that night I had a tarpon trip and we hooked a big one about 130 pounds outside of Government Cut. He came inside the cut and got on the sandbar. This one also jumped in the boat and his head landed on my seat, the same seat that had blocked Daniel and me. His head was on the seat and his body was on the covering board and I had to lift him off the seat and push him back over the side.

177

But can you imagine a sailfish coming in the boat and a tarpon coming in the boat both in the same day. Those fish were really desperate to spend some time with us that day many years ago.

Trisha and the Remora

We're all entitled to make a mistake now and then. One of my most embarrassing happened on a charter years ago. For twenty years I ran my boat alone with no mate. For a good part of that time I kept my boat at Keystone Point Marina in North Miami. As circumstances developed the marina became owned and operated by a young lady in her early twenties by the name of Trisha Hamilton. Trisha had fished with me since she was a teenager as her father owned the marina and I operated out of there. After her father passed she took over full operation.

One summer day she chartered the boat with a couple of her girlfriends to go out in search of mahi mahis. We had a great day. The girls were having fun because we saw a lot of bottlenose dolphins, but not too much on the mahi mahi scene. At one point we caught a big remora, also known as a shark sucker, a fish that could be anywhere from a couple of inches long to three feet long. They have a big suction cup on top of their head that's used to latch onto whales, and turtles, and sharks. There's a specie that hangs on marlins, and another that hangs on sailfish. Occasionally they will even latch on to a boat. The bottom line is we caught one and brought it into the boat and I was explaining to the girls about the suction cup.

179

Just in passing I said to one of the girls, "Why don't you let it suck onto your leg? It'll make an interesting picture."

Sure enough she allowed us to put the remora onto her thigh. It latched on there and got a good grip and held on real tight. Eventually we took it off and to my embarrassment it left a huge mark much like a hickey would be. What had happened was that on the remora, I had never paid that much attention, but on the ring on the outside of the suction cup and on each of the power latches on the suction cup, it was a relatively rough surface. I guess that was there to remove slime so it could get a good grip on the fish it was riding along with. But it left this mark that was about four inches by two inches oval on this beautiful thigh. I was so embarrassed. Here was this beautiful girl with this great big mark on the side of her leg.

We learned a lot about remoras from that. We still stick them on the guys once in a while, but I make it a point to never stick them to a girl. Beware of the shark sucker. It can be very embarrassing if you're not careful where you put it. And by the way, they have been known to stick on to swimmers while they're diving offshore.

Used and Abused

I'd like to share a few observations I've made over the years that might influence your decision to release a fish. We used to fish some shallow artificial reefs off the Fontainebleau Hotel. We were literally the only boat that fished there. Even the charter boats rarely hit these spots for barracudas, even though these wrecks were loaded with them. I had numerous customers from up north who would spend hours on end casting tube lures and catching barracudas. Occasionally an amberjack would appear and we would pitch him a live bait. There were other species, but mostly we caught barracudas, and we had a ball. I can't help but think of the Gary Leff family, and Bob Evans and Harold Wallace. They were great trips just catching barracudas one after another. The significant thing I remember about those barracudas was that there was this one particular barracuda that was about seven or eight pounds. It had a gill raker that was torn out and literally hung out of the gill plate. The gill raker on a fish is much like a part of the lungs on a human being. They bleed profusely and are a critical part of the respiratory system. I caught this barracuda time, and time, and time again; and caught him and released him, and caught him and released him again, like we do with all our barracudas. We slowed down fishing there and no one knows what happened to him, but I saw him for months on end with that gill raker hanging out and he had no problems.

I caught a snook in Government Cut that had the same situation with the gill raker hanging out the back of his gill plate, and again, he was doing just fine, no strain, no pain, even though this critical breathing apparatus had obviously been damaged.

Probably the most shockingly damaged fish I ever caught was a white marlin. We caught this seventy-pound white marlin on my dad's boat. We were trolling offshore with guests of my dad. The amazing thing about this fish was somehow he had been cut from the lateral line around the bottom of his internal organs, and up to the lateral line. I don't mean just a scratch, I mean all the way through his protective wall. I could take my fingers and hook them over this cut on his left side, rub all the way around to his right side, either facing my fingers forward or aft, and could look at all his internal organs right there suspended inside his cut open body. It was unbelievable this critter was alive. And he fought like crazy, and jumped and everything else. This was totally scarred over, but from lateral line all the way under the fish to the lateral line the whole stomach area was completely cut open with his stomach and other vital organs just sitting out in the open. It's a wonder the remoras didn't drive him crazy.

Now I think back to another fish that I caught that involved my dad. I had my dad's best friend, Julian Gailin, out and we caught a sailfish that had the whole top if his back cut off. From behind his dorsal fin all the way to the front of his dorsal fin was completely cut off. Probably somewhere between five to eight percent of the depth of this fish from belly to back, that part was completely cut off and all scar tissue. You wonder how these fish survive these crazy things.

Then I recall a silky shark that was hundreds of pounds, and had packing straps wrapped all the way around its body cutting into it to where the shark had literally overgrown the packing strap.

In the 70s I caught an amberjack off Ft. Lauderdale in 325 feet of water and we brought it up from the bottom. We tagged it and released it, but it wouldn't go down. So my mate gaffed it in the belly to let the air out, and we released it again, but it still wouldn't go down. Long story short, my mate gaffed it seven times in the stomach region to get the air to go out, and we released it seven times. Finally we got the air out and it went down. Forty-eight hours later on the same wreck we caught the same amberjack by the same method and it seemed totally unfazed by the seven holes in its stomach.

It's just amazing how durable a fish can be. It really exemplifies how important catch and release can be. Even if a fish doesn't look too healthy, the fish has a better chance being released than it does in the fish box. When you're trying to decide to let a fish go or throw him in the box, none of them live on the dock; they all have a better chance in the open ocean.

Saltwater Sportsman

I have been doing seminars since 1984. I was lucky enough way back then to be invited by George Poveromo and Mark Sosin to do their seminar series. It could range anywhere from speaking in Miami to going to Chicago, Atlantic City, Houston, New Orleans, down in the Keys, and a lot of other great places. There were a few challenges over the years working with George and Mark. The first one that comes to mind was the great debacle in Chicago.

George and Mark had spoken with the fishing editor of the Chicago Tribune and he had talked them into doing a seminar up there. He was going to hype it up to get their auditorium full of people. They had booked a beautiful theater, made all the arrangements, and hired speakers and the support team to come in from all over the country. Then the outdoor writer had a heart attack. He was laid up and couldn't do any promotions. When the time came for the seminar we all went to this beautiful theater with plush red chairs. I honestly believe there were more people on the staff than there were in the audience. George told me the people in the audience outnumbered the people on the stage by two. But that's his recollection, and we're all entitled to our own. The bottom line was it was a regrettable program when it came to supporting the fishing industry, as there was no turnout for these great speakers. But we did our job and entertained those who were there, gave them a lot of good fishing information.

When the day was done we went back to our hotel. We were all meeting in the hotel restaurant for dinner. Looking out the windows it was a beautiful snowfall, and the restaurant was full of Christmas parties. There was a wandering violinist who was playing Christmas songs, either his songs or by requests. So he came to our table and asked if we had any requests, and I said, "How about playing Silent Night." So he started playing Silent Night and I started singing along with him. Still to this day nearly forty years later George still picks on me teasing Siiiilent Night, Hoooly Night... That was a real fiasco.

Another interesting challenge I had was when I was on my way to a seminar with George in Orlando right outside of Disneyworld. I lived in Pembroke Pines at the time so my wife, Ruth, and my son, Terry, and I were going to drive up on Friday night. I would do the seminar all day on Saturday while they went to one of the amusement parks and would meet me later. We would all do something on Sunday and then head home Sunday night.

We left out of Pembroke Pines about 6:00 p.m. on Friday night and headed up the Florida Turnpike. When we got to around Stewart I had seen this truck a couple of times with a bed tied to the back of it. At any rate, I went over this rise and there on the road in front of me was a box spring. There was a semi on my left and cars on my tail, and we were doing seventy miles an hour. In my Windstar I had only one choice, and that was to try to drive over the box springs, straddling the wood so I wouldn't blow out my tires. I guess I made it straddling the box springs, but it tore open my gas tank and got caught underneath my car. So I was dragging the box springs with nails dragging on the asphalt, sparks flying all over the place, gas pouring out of my gas tank, and flames shooting out behind me. The semi next to me was honking; the car behind me was honking, and I was looking out the rear view mirror at the flames coming out the rear of the car with my wife and my son in the car with me. So I told them that when I stopped, don't grab anything; just get out of the car and run. As I slowed down I pulled off the side of the road onto the grass, which fortunately stopped the sparks, and I guess the gas tank was about empty. The bottom line is we stopped and baled out, and there was no more fire. Here we were on the side of the Florida Turnpike at seven o'clock at night with no gas tank and quite a fiasco. I finally got a tow truck to tow me back to Hollywood to my sister and brother-in-law's. I borrowed his truck to drive back to Orlando while his auto repair shop would replace my gas tank.

So we got in his truck and headed back to Orlando. I arrived there at 5:45 in the morning, got the family checked into the hotel, and by the time I was done with that it was time to report into the seminar. I told George that if I fell asleep on the stage just to poke me in the ribs and I would be good to go. I must add, I did fall asleep a few times during the day, but we managed to get through the seminar, and it was an interesting day to say the least.

We had another seminar in Atlanta, Georgia. When George asked me to go, Terry, who was about ten or eleven years old at the time, was listening in on the phone. He said, "If you're going to Atlanta in January I want to go with you because it's going to snow, and I've never seen snow."

I said, "It almost never snows in Atlanta, so you won't have to go with me. But if it's snowing in Atlanta when it's time for me to go, you can go too." On this day in January I fished all day and cleaned up, ran to the airport, and flew to Atlanta. I got out of the airport and hailed a cab. While we were driving to the hotel the cabbie said, "Boy, it's going to be a real mess here tomorrow afternoon."

I asked, "Why is that?"

He said, "Right in the afternoon rush hour it's going to be snowing, and these people don't know how to drive in the snow."

I said, "Oh don't tell me it's going to snow. Please. If it's snowing I was supposed to bring my son, and I didn't bring him.'

He said, "Well, there's an awful good chance you'll be seeing snow tomorrow afternoon."

I did the seminar, and sure enough when I came out in the afternoon there was light snowfall. My very good friend, Gary Leff, had been at the seminar and he picked me up to take me home to his house to spend the weekend. We planned to go fishing on Sunday. Well, the snow canceled the fishing for Sunday, but as we sat in his family room on Saturday night we had the back porch light on and it was a beautiful winter scene; snowflakes falling, snow capped hand railings, it was right out of a famous artwork of a winter scene.

I called home and talked to my wife. She told me not to tell my son that it was snowing. I said, "Well, I can't lie to him." But he heard her say that it was snowing, so I didn't have to tell him it was snowing, he already knew.

So he got on the phone, "It's snowing, isn't it Dad."

I said, "Yeah, it's snowing, but don't you make trouble for your mother."

He said, "You told me if it was snowing I could go with you."

I said, "Well, I didn't realize it was going to snow, and now it's too late. And don't make trouble for your mother."

I got off the phone and Gary said, "Why don't you bring your son up here to play in the snow tomorrow?"

I said, "I'd love to, but that could be awful expensive."

So Gary called the airline and talked to them for a while. He finally put his hand over the mouthpiece and said, "It's $750 each way to fly your son up and back to see the snow."

I said, "No, that won't work. I can't do it."

So he hung up. Then he got serious. He got out his violin (figuratively) and called the airline again. He said that if I were to die in Atlanta they would give the family a special rate to come to Atlanta. But I was in Atlanta teaching Georgia residents lessons on how to fish and make their life better. I was doing a public service to the people of Atlanta, so the airline, based in Atlanta, should reciprocate and give us a deal on a ticket to Atlanta. Finally after several minutes of playing his violin and begging, he put his hand over the mouthpiece and said, "$200 round trip."

I said, "Book it, Dano."

So he booked a flight for 7:30 the following morning to fly my son to Atlanta. I called my wife and told her that we had booked a flight for Terry to fly up in the morning, and he needs to be at the airport at 6:30. She said, "Well, if he's coming, I want to come."

I said, "If you come, it's $1,500. If he comes, it's $200."

She said, "Well, I'm going to the mall. It's going to be more expensive for you, but that would be my choice."

I said, "OK, have a ball." So my son was flying up in the morning. Gary and I got up to go pick him up at the airport. I had to bust a gut listening to Gary. We were on the north side of Atlanta, and the airport is on the south side. So we got out on the expressway loop in the morning and there was plenty of snow on the ground. We were driving about thirty miles an hour and a car went flying by.

Gary said, "Man those people are going to kill themselves. These people don't know how to drive in the snow." What Gary didn't notice was that the license plate on the car was from Wisconsin. And another car went flying by and Gary went into a tirade again. That one was from Michigan. And another car whizzed by and Gary went into another tirade. Minnesota. I had to chuckle. Gary was screaming and hollering about these people driving too fast in the snow, and yet all the people speeding were from snow country where they were very familiar with the conditions. Granted, the people from Atlanta were diving very slow, but the tourists from the north headed for Miami had no problem dealing with the snow. They do it every year, all winter long.

We picked up Terry at the airport and stopped on the side of the road where the snow had drifted up into nice piles where Terry could play in it. We went to downtown Atlanta where everybody on the hill shared all their devices with Terry as he went down the hill on sheets of cardboard, plastic dishes, toboggans, sleds, and just had an absolute ball all day. In the afternoon we went to Gary's house and Terry made a red snowman where the red Georgia clay was mixed with the snow. Then Gary took us to the airport and we flew back to Miami. What a memorable trip that was.

At one of Saltwater Sportsman's early seminars in Miami, I will always remember Mark Hufftelling was one of the speakers. Mark was a fireman for Dade County and we were in one of the halls at the University of Miami doing our seminar. As it turned out, it was perfect seminar weather. The wind was blowing thirty to thirty-five with intermittent rain. Nobody in their right mind wanted to go out in their boat. It was in the early days of the seminars. The seminars were just old enough to be very popular, but young enough to still draw huge crowds. So here we were at this hall and it was filling up. Then it was full. Then they were putting chairs backstage so people could glean a little bit of information.

Then here came the fire department saying, "You can't overload the auditorium. It's a safety hazard. You have to shut it down and remove fifty people."

Mark Hufftelling went to the firemen and said, "I've got this under control. I've done a headcount and we're just below capacity and we will shut it down at capacity." We went ahead and had a phenomenal seminar. We still talk about the weather that took place at the University of Miami seminar that year.

I've had some great times, both George and Mark together in the early days, and George in the latter years. The saltwater Sportsman National Seminar series has taught so many people so much about the sport of fishing that it's an icon in the industry and I'm proud to be involved in it.

Wrong Way Snook

I will start by saying that cast netting snook to harvest them is greatly illegal. It was September and the sardines were packed underneath Haulover Bridge on the north end of Miami Beach. We were casting Rapalas for tarpon and snook up current into the light, and winding them down current into the dark where the shadows where. The sardines were stacked up. Periodically we'd catch a snook or tarpon, or at least hook one. Some we would catch, some we would lose, but the fishing was really good, and the excitement level was high with the snook and tarpon smashing into the schools of sardines. It was crazy.

A car pulled in and parked under the bridge about forty feet from the water. Two kids got out of the car with a paper shopping bag. They ripped it open and threw the bag on the ground and pulled out a plastic bag. They opened the plastic bag and pulled out a cast net, threw the plastic bag on the ground, and set up the net. They walked over to the seawall and threw the cast net on the school of sardines and came up with a ten-pound snook and a bunch of sardines. By the time they got the snook out of the net, the sardines were all beat to death. They threw the cast net again came up with two snook, one probably seven or eight pounds, and one about twelve pounds. By the time they got the snook out of the net, the net

191

was a mess and the sardines were all dead and now they had three snook lying in the sand.

They squared the net away the best they could and threw it again and caught another ten-pound snook. They left the cast net lying in the sand, picked up the four snook and threw them in the trunk of the car and drove away leaving their mess of dead sardines, the cast net, and the plastic bags for the rest of the world to take care of while they went home with their four illegal snook.

It didn't take them long to catch their limit, but there weren't any ethics involved there.

Englishmen Tarpon Fishing

The British come down and tarpon fish with us from time to time, and the ones I have known have been more selective than their American counterparts. There was a time when we would kill a lot of tarpon when people wanted to have them mounted. Then Pflueger Taxidermy decided they would no longer stuff tarpon; they would only make fiberglass reproductions. They actually gave us a bonus commission if we didn't kill any tarpon, but instead got people to do release mounts on them. So we got in the habit of not killing tarpon.

When we got onto a big boat we had to leave the tarpon in the water because we couldn't bring them in the boat. A lot of times we would gaff them in the lower lip and lift them part way up out of the water and take a picture. That worked for most of our people. Once in a while someone would get upset about not pulling them in the boat, so we had to tell them that the fish were too heavy to pull into the boat without doing great harm to them and risking harm to the people on the boat. It became a no brainer that tarpon stayed outside the boat.

I had this series of charters from England, and these fishermen felt that if they weren't in the picture with the fish, then they really hadn't caught the fish. So we did all our tarpon fishing with them centered on the fact that we would catch the tarpon somewhere where we could swim the tarpon to a beach and the anglers would get in the water with their fish. As an example, at Haulover Inlet, instead of fishing in the ocean for the ocean tarpon, we would fish in the bay with dead baits over near the drift boat docks. We would wind the tarpon up to the boat and then swim it over to the sandbar. The angler would jump in the water and get his arms under the tarpon. He would pick it up and have his picture taken, and put the tarpon back in the water. Then his arms and his shirt would be covered with this goopy, disgusting slime. They'd have their picture and then walk the tarpon around to revive it, and it would be no worse for wear.

When I tell this story I recall the time we caught a 150-pound tarpon and swam it over to the sandbar and got the pictures. When the angler released the fish it swam a few feet away and rolled over and sank to the bottom. So they picked it up and they walked it and walked it, but they just couldn't revive this fish. I don't know if it had a bad heart or what happened, but it wouldn't revive or survive. As I understand it, a mounted tarpon replica still hangs in a tackle shop in Southern England. Because it wouldn't survive they had the fish mounted and sent back to England. At least it had a final resting place that was worthy of it.

Those British anglers were pretty interesting though. Where most of our anglers are thrilled to hook a tarpon, when they hook a stingray or leopard ray they complain about not catching the tarpon they were targeting. Likewise, the British anglers who were not so used to this kind of fishing would catch a 150-pound ray and be absolutely thrilled. And we caught a lot of them. We would grab them by their air holes behind their eyes and lift them up onto the covering board and get a picture with them.

The stingrays fought by running around, going down and anchoring themselves on the bottom. We would have to maneuver around and lift and lift, and if we could reach the leader we could break them loose from the bottom, but they would fight all over the place. Their only saving grace was that they made some good runs, and they were a popular fish back in England.

The leopard rays on the other hand, a beautiful fish, black with white spots, would run all over the bay. They would jump and never hung on the bottom. They were a mid-level fish, probably as beautiful as any sea creature you could ever catch. And they were a little more dangerous because they were also capable of jumping into the boat. For some reason they would uniquely land up on the bow, which was a small, limited lower space. But they'd land on the lower deck or on the seat, and we'd hurriedly throw them back overboard and go back to fighting them. But what a beautiful fish. They fought a lot like a tarpon – two or three jumps out of most of them, and they never sucked down on the bottom. They fought very hard, took great runs, and were really a treat to catch. We never had to worry about swimming them over to a sandbar and putting an angler in the water with them.

We caught some of those tarpon at the south end of Key Biscayne and had to swim them over to the trout flats and pick them up off the nasty weedy bottom. Those Englishmen loved to catch their tarpons, stingrays, and leopard rays, but they always wanted to get in the water with their tarpon. Now, when I see bull sharks eating some of those tarpon, I don't think I'd like to see my clients jumping into the water with them anymore.

I'd Rather be Lucky and Good

Somebody asked me recently if I've ever had some scary moments in boating, so I figured I share a few.

The first one that comes to mind happened when I was up at the Fort Lauderdale Billfish Tournament. It was a very nasty Friday morning. We were headed out of the inlet on the outgoing tide and a strong east wind. There was a Contender boat in front of us, and he hit a sea and ended up standing so vertical that we could see every screw head across the back of his deck. He was pointed right straight up in the air; how much further he could have gone up without flipping over backwards, I don't know, but we were all in amazement.

That should have been a warning to us, and we probably should have paid better attention, but I'm sure we were distracted by that boat having stood on its tail. The same wave that they stood up on broke down on top of the bow of my Dusky 256. The sea came right over the top of my windshield and filled the boat with water. My brother-in-law, Joe, was in the back of the boat scrambling around on his hands and knees keeping the scuppers clear so the water could run out the back of the boat. We had so much water in the boat that I think it ran over the back of the transom, but then it ran out of the scuppers. We got out of the inlet and survived

196

a day of fishing, but to see that Contender stand right straight up, and then have that wave break over our bow, that was an eye opening experience never to be forgotten.

I guess tournaments put us in some harrowing situations that we wouldn't normally be in most of the time. We pay a lot of money to get in the tournaments, and if it's a go, we gotta go too. I had the Cotrone bothers on the boat fishing the Pompano Rodeo. We were going in Hillsboro Inlet, and again it was an outgoing tide with an east wind – always the worst of conditions. I was going in the inlet when we got picked up by the sea. I had both engines screaming in reverse to keep from ramming into the jetties. I was in definite fear for Ben Cotrone because he was sleeping down in the cabin, and if we had hit those rocks there was no telling what might happen to him. But fortunately I got the boat stopped in time. Those Evinrudes are so dependable. They hung in there tough under the worst of circumstances.

And as I tell this story now I think of another really crazy one. We were coming into Miami Beach Marina heading northwest. There was a boat coming southeast and we were set up to pass port to port. Just as we were approaching the opening to the marina this boat that was going in the opposite direction hung a hard left turn right in front of us. Again those Evinrudes hung in there. I was going 4000 RPMs in forward and instantly I was wide open in reverse. 4000 in forward, to however many RPMs the engines can take going in reverse, and the engines never missed a beat. We missed that boat just by inches. It was close to a disaster. I don't know what that other captain was thinking, but he was in a great position to kill a lot of people. If it weren't for those Evinrudes we would have been in a heap of trouble.

Then there's the worst one of them all. Abie Raymond and I had been in Bimini for several days with the Panter family that flew over in their own plane. They had flown home and Abie and I ran home. It was a relatively good trip, three to five foot seas, maybe four to six, but it was down sea. We had done it with no incidents in a couple of hours. When I got about a mile off Government Cut I called my sister, Sue, to tell her we would be in shortly. She liked to come down and see us when we came in. We were on the north side of the inlet and it had gotten rougher as we came closer to shore. When we were about a half-mile offshore, the wave we were on just disappeared and we crashed into the wave ahead of us. The water that came over the bow was so violent that it shattered my plexiglass windshield. I got a bump on my head from the plexiglass as it went by. When the water stopped washing through the boat Abie had one leg inside the boat and one leg outside the boat, one arm inside the boat, and one outside. He was straddling the starboard covering board. The water was so deep that the boat was rolling from side to side. He would run back and forth across the back of the boat to counterbalance the load as the water sloshed from side-to-side. I put out a call to the Coast Guard that we were full of water and in danger of losing the boat. I kept going forward slowly toward the beach. We were in calmer water now, and the bilge pumps worked and Abie worked; the scuppers were clear and all the water ran out. We were none the worse for wear, but boy, that was a lot of water in the boat. The thing I think about that was thank God there were no passengers on board. And the interesting thing about it, another professional captain who ran a big boat at the marina, took his guests out on a thirty-five foot runabout exactly one week later, and exactly the same weather conditions. He stuffed the bow of this runabout going down sea and shattered his windshield and several people on his boat were severely cut by the windshield washing past them. It points out how lucky we were that we got through it with no major issues. Even the best of us have to be ever vigilant because we never know when a wave is going to catch up with us.

So, that was my worst one, but I do remember one other one that was pretty crazy. I've talked in the past about going from Clarencetown, Long Island, to West Caicos where the seas were horrific. And I talked about my harrowing voyage from Cozumel to Key West with the hallucination of the pelican coming onto the bow. I had a Miami Beach Rod and Reel Tournament to fish in Bimini. Ray Storemont and Buddy Yarborough were going to go across with me, and Dixie Burns was going to fly over. So Dixie gave all of her tackle to Ray to bring to the boat. We talked on the phone several times questioning should we go or not go. OK, well let's take a look. But when I got there in the morning they had already loaded all their gear up. So I loaded my gear too.

We were on my Dusky 256 fish around cuddy cabin and I said, "OK, we'll go out to the sea buoy and we'll see how it looks." So we beat our way out to the sea buoy, blowing like crazy in four to six foot seas. We got to the sea buoy, and it hadn't gotten any worse out there. The wind and water were going generally in the same direction. We questioned if we should go but we figured, well, we're already here and we've got everything loaded, so let's keep going. We kept going, but it was a harrowing trip. We went through vicious thunderstorms, and the wind just kept blowing a horror, probably thirty-five to forty. The seas were about five to eight feet. I would power up over a wave and then slow down. And power up over the next wave and slow down again. We went that way for hours on end. I don't know how long it was, but we beat our way across to Bimini and tied up at Seacrest and everyone asked, "Where in the world did you come from?"

I said, "Well we came from Miami."

"You couldn't have come from Miami. No man in his right mind would have left from Miami." Everybody on the dock was totally shocked that we came across. Dixie's tackle and her tackle bag were just full to the brim with seawater. Everything was soaking wet and we were like three drowned rats. The interesting thing is, nobody else came across.

We were the only people around and I netted some pilchards in a canal. We went just south of the Sunshine Inn because it was the only place calm enough to fish behind the rocks. We caught giant mutton snappers and giant horse eyed jacks. We were looking at downtown Bimini right in front of us and doing some phenomenal fishing, while nobody else was in sight because the weather was so bad. I guess if you're going to be dumb, you've got to be tough, and a little luck helps too.

Now this reminds me of one more story of long voyages. I was going from Haulover Inlet to Bimini with Randy Lacey. We might have had Dan Fulmer on the boat. But we had a load of lumber to work on Randy's house. We were on the forty-eight foot Lemay built *Top Luck*. We shoved off about four in the afternoon. It was an east-northeast wind and it was rough with huge seas at night. I couldn't see the compass and it didn't have a light in it. In breaks in the weather I'd grab my Zippo lighter and flick it enough so I could see the compass, and I would be headed too far to the north. I would turn to the south enough to be on course again and in short order I would check the compass again and I'd be headed too far north. I kept doing this and I'd turn south and the seas would turn the boat too far north. I went that way for hours on end.

When we got to Bimini we were going to the residential canal. So we finally got up to the house and tied up. Jean Lacey was standing on the dock waiting for us. I had time to dry off a little coming down the canal. I came down off the bridge and ss I came down Jean cracked up laughing.

I said, "What's the matter?"

She said, "You must have been scared stiff out there."

I said, "Why's that?"

She said, "Your face is white as snow."

I scratched my face and my fingernails were buried in caked up salt. I had been taking so much seawater over the bow that my face had slowly built up so much salt that my face was completely white. I think it took me an hour in the shower to get the salt out of my hair that night, but what a long trip that was to Bimini.

Those are some stories of some times I should not have been there, but thank God I was lucky as well as good.

The Moon and the Wind - Tides and Eddies

So let's take a look at the moon, the sun, and the weather. Probably the thing that Abie and I watch the most day in and day out, because it has an influence at different times everyday is: what's the moon doing? We know from years of fishing that when the moon hits the horizon, the fish tend to bite. I like rising better than setting, but they both have pretty strong effects. We have proven this time and time again with swordfish, sailfish, tarpon, and kingfish. You want to be in the right place when the moon is at the horizon. That means that if you're thinking about pulling up your swordfish baits and running for an hour to another spot, don't do it right when the moon is about to come up. If you're going to have to wait a half hour on the same drift, stick to that drift because it might make your whole day. The swordfish bite when the moon is on the horizon. I don't know why it happens. They call them solunar events and they hold true in hunting, fishing, everything. So always have your baits in the water at moonrise. There are any number of apps you can get for your phone that will tell you the time for moonrise everyday.

That being said, beyond moonrise, six hours later the moon will be straight overhead. Or if it was the moonset, six hours later the moon will be straight under your feet. In solunar tables this is called the major feeding period. It lasts longer, but not is as intense as the moon at the horizon, which is called the minor feeding period.

I honestly one day predicted a swordfish bite when I knew the moon was directly under feet, I mean within ten minutes. Then there was a lull in the fishing for hours, and I predicted within five minutes when the fish would start biting again, and that was within twenty minutes of our best catch of the day. We caught two swordfish that day. We caught one with the moon directly underfoot, and one just after, but very close to moonrise. Take it to the bank, that moon will have an awful lot to do with your fishing.

Also, the moon will tell you what the tide is doing. If it's a full moon, high tide is going to be somewhere around eight or nine o'clock in the morning. It'll be true every week. Then you want to plan a second fishing trip. Say you're in Snake Bight and the tide was falling and you did really well, so you want to know when you can replicate the same time of day and the same tide. The answer is two weeks and one hour later you'll have exactly the same conditions. It'll be a different moon phase, and the wind might be from a different direction, but at least the same time of day the tide will be falling again. Again, that's two weeks and one hour later. So that might come in handy somewhere in your planning.

That being said, the next thing we want to look at is what's the weather doing? Well, there's a cold front up around Tennessee, and we start to get a south wind and the barometer just begins to drop. This is a really good time to fish. As that wind comes around to the southwest we're getting very close to the bottoming out of the barometer. The fishing won't be as good because the barometer is bottoming out. But there are some fish that like this bottoming out barometer. The ones I think of are bottom fish, kingfish, and sharks. They like that southwest to west wind. Conversely fish like dolphin and sailfish will bite on the south wind, and will shut off as soon as it goes to the west. Another fish that loves it, even in the rain, prior to the front coming all the way through, are tarpon. They love it.

When the front goes through and we have a northwest wind without a cloud in the sky, fishing can be really tough. Bluebird days, the most beautiful days in the world, the barometer is very high, therefore there's lots of pressure on the fish, and they just want to chill. They're just like us, it's a nice cool day, the sun is out, the birds are singing – we might as well take a nap. Some fish take a nap too. This is a really hard time to catch fish. Fortunately we have found that under these conditions, when the sailfish won't bite, for some reason the tarpon do. Sometimes this will be a good condition for Spanish mackerel too.

On the offshore scene you might be able to catch a couple of bottom fish. It could be a good time to troll for groupers on the reef, because with the calm water and the cool temperature, the water will tend to be very clear on the reef and you can troll for groupers in fifteen to thirty feet of water. As the front gets farther away and the barometer starts to drop again, here comes the northeast wind and some cloud cover, and all of a sudden everything turns on. The sailfish are biting, the dolphin are biting, the Spanish mackerel are biting. Everything loves that northeast to east wind. A little bit of a falling barometer and some clouds in the sky make for an exciting time to fish. Albeit it, it might be a little rougher, but it's a good time to find a way to get offshore.

I used to have a situation where I lived way inland. When I got closer to the coast and had already eaten breakfast and had a cup of coffee, I got to the tackle shop and got out of the truck, and the wind was blowing out of the northeast at fifteen to twenty. By the time I was done buying my chum and my bait for the day, I would be losing my breakfast next to a cocoanut tree because I was so fired up that we were going to have a great day of dolphin, and sailfish, and kingfish, and tunas.

Weather can have a great deal of bearing on fishing. If you've got a few clouds, you're probably going to have better fishing than on a bluebird perfect day. If you've got a southwest wind, an awful lot of times you're going to have to resort to the eating kind of fish instead of game fish, because most of those kingfish and groupers will be biting a lot better than sailfish.

Tides and Eddies

Let's touch on the tide. If you're fishing in an inlet and the tide is going out, meaning the water is going from the bay to the ocean, on the outgoing tide the predator fish will congregate along the edges of the main channels, especially around ambush points like piers, docks, rock outcroppings, drop offs, and dredging flaws. They will be looking for the bait moving from the bay to the ocean. You'll have far more action if you're drifting your live baits or casting your lures as you drift along with the tide, and wind the lures down tide as you're going out the inlet.

Conversely, on the incoming tide, the current comes down or up the beaches and sweeps around the ends of the jetties. A high percentage of the fish will be lying on the outside of the jetties near the ends as the water and bait crash against the jetty, sweep out toward the end, and then out and around the end of the jetty. There will be some fish along the jetties expecting the bait to be coming in with the tide, but that will be a much lesser population of fish. So it's very obvious, there is the inlet, and there is the tide, no brainer.

But what about when you want to move offshore a little bit? If it's the wintertime and you're in the Keys, or somewhere else in South Florida, bear in mind that there are periodic shrimp runs. On the outgoing tide, early in the morning, all these shrimp are coming out of the bays and inlets and into the ocean. These shrimp are feeding mackerel, snappers, snook, tarpon, and groupers. There's all kinds of stuff offshore of the inlets eating on shrimp. So taking some shrimp in the wintertime on a daytime trip can be a good investment. It can really make your day, especially if you get out there on the beginning of the outgoing tide.

Then as you move farther offshore, you've still got an incoming or outgoing tide and you can run into situations with color changes. As an example, while fishing for kingfish off Haulover Inlet we would have very nice, clean water in ninety feet. Right in front of the inlet, as the tide started to push out, here would come this brown water edge. That brown water edge would shut those kingfish right off in that location. On the outgoing tide what happens is the fresh water pushes out onto the reef and sometimes beyond. That can create a nice rip, or color change in 90, or 120, or 180, or 250 feet of water. It'll go from some fresh water, and some dirty water, up against beautiful Gulf Stream water, giving you a nice sharp rip and a great place to troll, or kite fish, or live bait. A rip is anywhere there is conflicting water densities and currents. When rips form, both the dirty water and the clean water run toward each other. When they collide they turn down. And when that water turns down it takes baitfish down the water column. So, while your sailfish will be up on the surface feeding on the flying fish on the clean side of the rip, that downturn of bait and nutrients fires up the kingfish that will be down in the mid water level taking advantage of what they find below the rip. This might mean that fish that were in shallower water were pushed out on this edge, and they all congregated in one line giving you a great place to begin searching.

Conversely, on the incoming tide, now all those edges are moving in over the top of the reef, and it's anybody's guess whether the dolphins, sailfish, kingfish, wahoo are going to be spread out whether from seventy-five to 250 feet, or congregating from 100 feet to 200 feet. You kind of have to guess and work with the other boats on the radio on the incoming tide, whereas the outgoing tide made it much easier to get on those fish. Those are the main considerations with an incoming and outgoing tide.

Where will the rips be? The outgoing tide gives you a much better definition. Low outgoing tide is really popular for wahoo, because it makes these sharp rips that might be in ninety feet of water south of the inlet, or 250 feet north of the inlet for example, but the bottom line is that if you troll up and down those rips and color changes, you've got a really good chance at a wahoo. If you live bait the same edges, you've got a really good chance for sailfish or dolphin. Kingfish also love to lie along a rip.

Now here's an important thing to remember. Rips can indicate a noticeable difference in the current. In the springtime sailfish are trying to get south to spawn. So if we have our springtime north current on the outside of that rip, a sailfish just swimming three knots trying to get south doesn't make any progress. So even sailfish will slip on the inside of a rip into the greener, slower water so they can make better time on their journey south. It's always a question which side of the rip is going to be the best for fishing. Usually it's the clean side, but if it isn't working for you, try the dirty side. You might also find out that the rip is only right on the surface, and the kingfish are still inside of it down below in that inshore water.

I hope this helps you to understand rips and currents. There's a lot to be said about the outgoing tide and the options are easier to define, but that doesn't mean you should go home on the incoming tide. We catch a lot of snook on the incoming tide, and a lot of sailfish and dolphin too.

Another issue related to currents, along the Florida coast, especially from Fowey Rocks north, are back eddies in the Gulf Stream. The Gulf Stream is coming up from the Keys. It curves around Ajax Reef and Fowey Rocks and turns north. In that stretch, because it goes offshore and turns to the north, we get a lot of back eddies. What happens with a back eddy is the Gulf Stream turns toward shore going west, then turns south paralleling the coast. After going south for five or ten miles it then turns offshore and eventually joins the northbound current. It goes in a circular motion roughly the shape of a paperclip. If you get off, say Miami Beach, and you're drifting toward shore very fast, and you have nice clean water, this is a prime area to find ocean predators. It's actually that back eddy of the Gulf Stream turning toward shore. So it's bringing all these offshore predators in toward the reef. There's a very high potential for great fishing.

That described the situation at the middle of Miami Beach, but if you get off Government Cut, and you have beautiful blue water and a south current, that's the back eddy running back to the south. It's liable to be in very shallow. In a blue water strong south current, most of the time the best fishing will be in very shallow. That's a great time to live bait in sixty or seventy feet of water. Watch out for showering ballyhoo or diving frigate birds. Fish that shallow water.

Then as you get down ten miles to the south, stop the boat and start to drift on a southeast wind. You're going east, upwind as you drift, and you're scratching your head, wondering what's happening. You are where that back eddy has looped around pushing offshore. This is the worst place to fish. The water is nasty and dirty, and it's rough. It's pushing water from inshore out towards the Gulf Stream. It's a bad place to fish, it's rougher, there are no fish there, and you've got to get out of it. Call a friend on the radio ten miles north and see if he has a south or north current. Or call a guy five or ten miles to the south and see if he's got a nice blue water edge pushing back in. But get out of that spot because it's not going to work very well.

One other tip, when you're in that south current, you might go offshore toward the outside edge of that clean water. You might find a little rip there with some grass in it where it went from green to blue. Now it will go to green again as that offshore current pushes around from where it's going out to the east and starting to curve back north with the Gulf Stream. There will be some green water there on the outside, and between that blue inshore water and the green offshore water sometimes you'll find some nice dolphin.

So keep these things in mind about the back eddies of the Gulf Stream, and they might help you produce some fish as well. Stay out of that current that's running towards the Gulf Stream, it'll be a tough time catching them there.

Tight lines and good fishing. I hope you're enjoying our books.

Al Pizza and Steve Roadruck Permit

We always hear so much about how spooky permit can be. I was out on my twenty-five foot Dusky with Al Piazza and Steve Roadruck. We were out for a good day of fishing, and as I remember it the fishing had been quite slow. We went by the Belzona Barge just to see if there were any African pompano there, even though we knew it was the wrong time of year. We saw these big flashes of light from the sides of fish, but we couldn't get any bites out of them. I kept trying to get a better idea of what they were and finally realized they were permit. I had some crabs in a bucket back at Miami Beach Marina, so we wound everything in and ran back to get them. We retrieved the crabs and ran back out to the Barge.

In relatively short order we caught a couple of permit. But then the permit went down and we were looking around for them. One of the guys had a crab on a rod, and I had wound it up and it was hanging behind the boat. I put the rod in the rod holder while we drove around dragging this crab only about ten feet behind the boat. We were just driving around trying to spot the permit again. When I turned around three permit were attacking the crab ten feet behind the outboard motor. We were trolling the crab and here were these allegedly spooky permit. It just shows to go you that permit aren't always as spooky as they are supposed to be.

We were in Bimini with Ray Stormont, and Dixie Burns, and Buddy Yarborough. We pulled up to a wreck and Ray went through his whole tackle box trying to get a bite, but all to no avail. Buddy said, "There they are," and fired a popping plug over to where they were. He started chugging his plug across the surface and a permit jumped all over it. That one cut us off on the wreck. We had one more popping plug, and Ray tried the same thing, chugging it across the surface, and once again the permit jumped all over it. It's amazing how much you can discover about fish in odd situations.

Tarpon in the Boat

One of the worst things that can happen in inshore fishing is to have a tarpon jump in the boat. It happened a few times with us, but several times they were very small fish and it was no big deal. But there were also a couple of real big ones.

The first real big one was during the Miami International Boat Show. I had met with Gary Walker from Penn in January and he had signed me on to be a Penn field tester. He gave me a whole set of twenty pound spinning rods and reels, twelve pound spinning outfits, eight pound spinning outfits; everything we needed to go fishing.

The boat show was the middle of February and I was out on a tarpon charter in the morning. In the afternoon I was going to hang out at the Penn booth. I had my first twenty-five foot Dusky and it had horizontal rod racks on both sides of the cockpit. On those rod racks I had three brand new twenty-pound spinning outfits and three brand new eight-pound outfits. We were using our Penn Internationals on conventional rods for tarpon fishing.

We were fishing along Bal Harbor Beach and hooked a nice tarpon that was putting up a good fight. One of the guests was standing there trying to get pictures while the other guest was fighting the fish. When I grabbed the leader the fish dove under the boat. I let it go. We were all facing south on the starboard side of the boat, and over on the port side in jumped this tarpon right into the boat. The cameraman jumped into the motor well, and the angler and I ran up to the bow. This tarpon was just thrashing around in the cockpit, beating everything to pieces like there was no tomorrow. Finally he settled down and I grabbed him by the lower jaw and threw him overboard and he took off swimming toward the beach. It would be a miracle if he survived because the cockpit was covered in scales and slime and mud. It was just a terrific mess.

I started throwing buckets of water on the slime and the rest of the mess when I looked at floor; there were pieces of fishing rods all over the place. When I took inventory of everything all three twenty pound rods were broken to pieces. On the reels the handles were bent, and the bails were broken. The outfits were totally wrecked. I looked to the other side of the boat and there were two eight-pound outfits broken with pieces lying on the deck. There was the tip of an eight-pound rod, but the bottom half and the reel were gone. Apparently the tarpon had kicked it overboard.

The next tarpon that jumped in the boat was with this young man named Ray who would come down from New Jersey to fish with me maybe two or three times a year. He used to come down to visit his grandmother and we would go tarpon fishing every time he came down. We always had a good time. We always caught tarpon and I think we caught a sailfish one time, but most of his trips were for tarpon fishing. Finally one time he brought his girlfriend and his grandmother with him. He said he was bringing them because his grandmother did not understand how I would go fishing and never bring anything home to eat.

213

We met at Miami Beach Marina and ran down the bay. We went fishing at the south end of Key Biscayne because that was where the tarpon had been biting the best. Nothing was happening there. There were no bites and nothing showed up. After having no success there I ran back up to Government Cut where I knew there were fish all over the place. It was an incoming tide so I knew with an incoming tide on the south side of Government Cut we should be able to get a pretty quick fight out of a tarpon and release it. We would hurry so we could catch and release him before he goes down inside the Cut toward downtown Miami. When that happens we'd have a long drawn out fight.

Having caught loads of tarpon here before, and having made our first drift, half way through the drift we hooked up on a tarpon. It was jumping and carrying on and fighting like crazy. We got a bunch of jumps out of it and headed over the dropoff. The leader came up and I brought it up, broke the leader and sent the tarpon on its way.

We turned to Grandma and Ray said, "Now you see why we go tarpon fishing. You see all the jumps and what a beautiful fish."

She said, "Sonny, I didn't see anything."

"OK, Grandma, maybe you'll get to see the next one."

We set up another drift and in very short order we got another tarpon on and it was jumping and carrying on and putting on a great show. Once again we got the leader up and the fish headed into the channel. I grabbed the leader and broke the fish off and Ray asked, "Well, Grandma, did you see that one?"

"No, I don't know what you're talking about. I didn't see anything."

Each time we caught a tarpon the girlfriend would be in the back of the boat taking pictures of the tarpon jumping. She was having a ball.

We hooked a third tarpon way back in almost as far as you can go on the south side of Government Cut by Fisher Island. This tarpon started swimming to the west along the bottom. It wasn't going toward the end of the jetties at all. The water was gin clear and we were watching the tarpon swimming down there. We were kind of at a stalemate, and we had the fish on long enough. It hadn't jumped and we couldn't get the leader up. It was just swimming along the bottom. It was a stalemate. All of a sudden that fish did an under roll. He turned around and headed back toward the bottom and came up and skyrocketed right into the boat right between Grandma and the girlfriend. The girlfriend jumped up on the fish box laying on her back with her arms and legs in the air. She was kind of screaming a little bit, and Grandma was on the back side of my seat at the front of the cockpit, screaming as the tarpon was thrashing in between them. I just reached over and grabbed Grandma under her arms and lifted her out of harms way. I helped her up to the bow of the boat and got her situated on the front seat.

Then I went back and the tarpon had settled down, so I helped the girlfriend across all the slime and the blood up to where she could get up to the front with Grandma. Then I went about cleaning up the boat as best I could. After I cleaned what I could, I brought the girls back to the back and Ray turned to his grandma and said, "Boy Grandma, now you can see how exciting this can be. But this was scary."

She said, "Sonny, I never want to go fishing again. I've seen enough. No thank you." And we called it a night.

215

I guess the lesson is that if you have a tarpon of any size jump into the boat, you're probably going to lose some tackle, and you're definitely going to shake up some people. But we've been lucky that when our tarpon have jumped in the boat that nobody has gotten hurt.

We had one more incident where a tarpon jumped in the boat on a night trip inside Haulover Inlet. We had hooked a tarpon in the ocean and followed it into the bay. This 130 pound tarpon jumped over the side of the boat and landed with is head on my seat. He was balanced on the side of the boat with his head on the seat. I put my hand under his head and pushed him back over the side. But he never came down into the boat where the disaster starts. It was a brief encounter of a peaceful kind.

I don't want any more tarpon jumping in the boat. It makes way too much mess.

Cape Cod

Over the years I've made several trips to Cape Cod pursuing striped bass, or bluefin tuna, or shark fishing. I have fond memories from there. My hosts on many occasions were Don and Sandy Blake. They had a large beautiful house in a quaint neighborhood with big trees in the town of Sandwich. The town was beautiful too. They were wonderful people and it was just a great place to visit.

When I stayed with them we went charter fishing one day and went around the tip of Monomoy Point, which is a giant sandbar located between Nantucket Sound and Cape Cod Bay. We went over some rips on the north side of the point, and using plug-casting tackle and rubber sluggos we would float them back in the rip and then jig them and catch these beautiful striped bass. What a pleasure it was. The action was fast and the fish were beautiful. Striped bass were always a tough fish for me to get connected to, but at this point this was some of the best striped bass fishing I had ever had. We caught numerous fish on light tackle and had lots of fun with artificial lures, just all you could ask for. When the tide slowed down and that fishery stopped, our captain took us back around to the south side, and there we found plenty of bird action. We caught striped bass and blue fish on really light tackle. These were much smaller fish but it was a lot of fun.

A couple of times I went to Cape Cod with Steve Nichols. Steve had his own twenty-five foot Dusky. The first year we went we charter fished out of Harish Port in Cape Cod, and we went way out to the east to fish for bluefin tuna. This was my first time doing that, and what an amazing event it was. We got out there trolling with spreader bars, like a big coat hanger rig. It's two dimensional. I would say the titanium bar is about three feet wide, and off the bars there were five strings of rubber squid. So there would be four squid on one string, and three squid on the next string, and then five squid down the middle, and then three, and then four. Some would be pink, or white, or blue, and then there was the one we called the clown because it was three colors. But there would only be one hook on each rig, and that was that fifth squid down the middle. Typically the bluefins would always attack the last squid down the line. It was a common predatory habit; always start at the back and work toward the front because the school could not see what was coming up behind them.

That day we were trolling among whales that were jumping, and with tails sticking up in the air. It was absolutely phenomenal, solid whales, solid birds, and we caught a whole bunch of tunas. Now the tunas that we were catching were around forty-five inches. If we had caught one over forty-seven inches we could have kept one more. We were allowed one under forty-seven inches and one over forty-seven inches, but all the ones we caught were under forty-seven inches. But what fun, and what great fighters. It was so neat to see all these baits behind the boat. It was so impressive; we'd have four or five lines out with nineteen squids on each rig. It was just unbelievable.

A couple of days later Steve and I went out again on a center console boat. Again we trolled spreader bars, but we didn't have much action that day. But the thing that was memorable was that at one point we put out heavy spinning tackle, and a diving plug, and I caught a beautiful bluefin tuna on this lighter tackle. This was an extra special treat. If only they had already discovered casting for bluefin tunas when I was young enough to do it. I can just imagine what it would be like to cast a popping plug or a sluggo, and have those tunas come crashing on top of my bait. Nonetheless the tuna fishing was really great.

As Steve Nichols and I progressed from there, the next time I went to Cape Cod we went out on his boat. It was slick glass calm, and we did see some tuna and some whales, but we didn't have any luck on the tuna grounds. What was really extra interesting about that trip was that Steve had gotten into doing some live baiting for the tunas. So he stopped at the Monomoy Point to catch bluefish for bait. We were in really shallow water and while I was casting for bluefish, the seals practically jumped in the boat trying to steal them off my line. It was absolutely crazy.

Then we took the bluefish out to the tuna grounds and we would send our live baits down toward the bottom. Before long we would start to get jerks on the line, and when we wound in our lines we would find a bluefish head, the whole spine, and a bluefish tail. The dogfish would attack the bait and eat the whole thing like a corn on the cob or an apple on the core. It was very frustrating. I remember Steve standing on the top of the cabin of his boat trying to spot the tunas in the water, but it just didn't pan out on that trip.

After that I went back to Cape Cod on another trip with Steve and we fished the famous Oak Bluff Shark Tournament. In that tournament it was Steve and one of his nephews and me. We had barrels of ground bluefish chum, and cases of big menhaden, and cases of dead bluefish for bait. We would run way offshore and set up these chum slicks with this bait. We caught a lot of blue sharks. There were so many that we got tired of catching these six, seven, and eight-foot sharks. On one of them I was holding the leader on a shark and took a wrap. He got really agitated and ripped the skin off the back of my hand. It was a very ugly mess. The first time we did that tournament all we caught was blue sharks.

The next time we fished the Oak Bluff Shark Tournament it was rougher than a cob. It was so rough that it was the only time in my life I ever went to the back of the boat and laid in a beanbag, wrapped up in my foul weather gear as we pounded our way offshore taking solid spray the whole time, soaking wet. It was also the only time in my life I ever experienced the beanbag, but I'll tell you what, if you haven't run in a beanbag at the back of a boat on a rough trip, you owe it to yourself because it is unbelievable how comfortable that beanbag is.

In that tournament we got out there and got lucky. We caught a nice big mako shark and tied it off in the water next to the boat. We called it in to the committee boat because they were sending a TV camera crew around to get action shots. So when the camera crew boat got there we boated our mako. It went crazy as we lifted it up the side of the boat, but we got it in. At the end of the tournament we weighed it, but we didn't quite come in the money. We had the second biggest mako, but there was no prize for that. The thresher sharks took all the top prizes. It was great that we got to catch a mako, but the biggest disappointment was that we went to all the trouble of waiting for the camera crew, and we hauled the shark into the boat on camera, but the only thing they showed on the TV was people getting seasick. It was so ridiculous that they centered the entire segment on the Oak Bluff Shark Tournament on seasickness instead of the great fish that were caught.

Such is life. Cape Cod is a beautiful place that offers some phenomenal fishing. We were tied up in the harbor and had baby bluefish and baby menhaden and striped bass all around the boat. I'll always have a sweet spot in my heart for Cape Cod. It was really a great place and I visited there with some great people.

Jesse Scams Al Hower on Mutton Snapper

Jesse Webb was the sales manager for Pflueger Taxidermy when they were bought by Shakespeare Corporation. Al Hower was moved down to be their Shakespeare fishing tackle representative in South Florida, and he had an office in the taxidermy office. Jesse took Al to Key West to go on the big springtime mutton snapper run, and the fishing was red hot. They caught kingfish, and grouper, and mutton snappers, and the whole shebang. Al was thrilled. He had come from Michigan and thought he had gone to heaven there were so many great fish. But he questioned why every time they caught a mutton snapper Jesse would check the rough side of the snapper. It would have a black spot and he would tell Al that if there was a black spot on the other side, then they were toxic to human beings and they couldn't eat them. So Jesse would check the left side and there would always be a black spot. He would check the right side and there would be a black spot there as well. He would throw them in the fish box and explain that although they were toxic to humans, they were no problem for his German shepherd. He would take them all and feed them to his dog.

They had this great trip to Key West and went home ecstatic with their grouper filets that they would share, and Jesse had all these filets to feed to his German shepherd. Then they went fishing in Key Largo. In the course of the day they caught several mutton snappers, and sure enough they had black spots on both sides, so Jesse took all the mutton snappers for his dog and Al only got to eat kingfish filets.

Then they went fishing in Miami and caught some more mutton snappers. At least this time Al got to eat some cobias. But doggone it; all the mutton snappers had black spots on each side, so Jesse took them home, supposedly to feed to his German shepherd. This went on for nearly a year. Finally Jesse got on the intercom at Pflueger Taxidermy and paged Al Hower and Jerry Webb to his office. They came into his office and Jesse said, "Al, I just can't do this anymore. I've had so much fun with this and so many great meals, but I have to share something with you. And I've got Jerry Webb here to protect me just in case you decide to erupt, but that black spot on one side of the mutton snapper being OK, and the ones with black spots on both sides being toxic, I wasn't being exactly truthful about that. But I have enjoyed eating more mutton snapper than I can ever remember. And I can't thank you enough, Al, but you gotta watch out for those old fishermen, they might come up with tales of what you can and can't eat, but they may not always be factual."

The Dry Dock

Back in the fifties and early sixties if you wanted to create an artificial reef off the coast of Florida you acquired something to sink and arranged to have someone tow it out to sea, and then you arranged to have somebody sink it. At the time we did not apply for permits, we just did it. But heaven forbid you get caught, because I guess even back then it was against the law. One of the guys who was doing a lot of that kind of work was Vince Spalding. He had a boat called the *Flying Fish* out of Pier Five and he advertised "No Fish, No Pay" on a sailfish or 200 pounds of fish. By sinking these wrecks off the coast, and for a long time he'd be the only one who knew where they were, he developed some spots where grouper and amberjacks congregated.

One of his projects was a dry dock that actually lifted ships out of the water off the west end of Government Cut. He acquired this de-commissioned dry dock, which is like a big sinkable, portable barge. He towed it out to 240 feet of water off Bear Cutoff the City of Miami.

I was fishing out of Haulover, and the Dry Dock was a pretty good run from there, but we were well aware of the wreck and how to find it. After Vince passed away, we got the numbers from our boss, Billy Miller, and we fished on it on numerous occasions. One time we even caught a 700-pound dusky shark there.

This other time we went down there to go shark fishing. We would sit on top of the wreck and put shark baits on the outriggers, while we also fished on the bottom. We were sitting on the Dry Dock and there was no wind, no current, and nothing was biting anywhere. Charlie Spiegel pulled up on the *Playmate*. He felt like he owned the Dry Dock because it was right in front of his marina. He was pretty possessive about it, but we kind of ignored it. Here we were, sitting next to each other, and neither one of us getting any bites. Our outrigger bait popped out of the rigger and the rod bent over and I took the boat ahead and Charlie calls over, "Yeah, go get your rigger bait."

My angler, Frank, was fighting and fighting this fish, and we were kind of going in a circle as we fought the fish. The way it was fighting it was kind of staying inside a circle. And right behind Charlie Spiegel's boat it popped to the surface. It was about a 140-pound Warsaw grouper. He was so mad he didn't even wait for his mate to wind in his lines. He took off running with his double-hooked bottom rig and five pound lead bouncing along the bottom, screaming and hollering at his mate as he went. We put the big grouper in the boat. It was the only thing we caught that day. Not only was it a good catch but it was a great incident as well.

Another time on the Dry Dock we were running the *Good Time IV*, which was owned by Billy Miller. And Billy Miller was running the *Rave* for Vera Shans. Billy had an all day charter on this rough and rainy day. We didn't have one. So Billy decided that the four crew members, Billy Miller, Gary Hall, Phil Conklin, and I would take the party out on the *Good Time I,V* and we would pay Vera Shans for the trip. We took off to go out fishing and ran down to the Dry Dock, and what a day it was! Oh my gosh. We caught two 100-pound groupers on the same rod at the same time. We caught a 240-pound grouper. We caught big sharks. It was one fish after another, the trip to never be forgotten. What a pile of monsters we caught that day on the Dry Dock with four crew members and one customer. It was a day to remember, and I still have the pictures to show what a great day it was.

Matt Bertuch

I used to fish by myself on my boat, just my customers and me. Then when I got the 33 Dusky I started taking a mate. We were out one day and it was Ron Jon Cook my mate, and a grandfather, father, and son on the boat, and me. The son's name was Matt Bertuch. We had a kite up on the starboard side of the boat and flat lines on the port side. It was one of those days where the flat lines were hot. We caught a couple of tunas and a couple of sailfish, all on the flat lines. Six-year-old Matt Bertuch came over to me and said, "Hey, Captain Bouncer, how long have you been fishing with that kite?"

I said, "Well, gee, Matt. We started fishing with it in the sixties, and now we're in the 2000s, so pretty close to forty years."

We kept on catching fish on the flat lines and after a while longer six year old Matt again asked, "Do you ever catch anything on that kite?"

"Yeah, Matt, we do catch a lot of fish on it." As the day progressed we did catch a couple of fish on the kite. At the end of the day the most notable fish was a thirty-pound kingfish. It skyrocketed on the bait, and it had a big old mark on its side like someone had taken an iron from an ironing board and pushed it against the skin. As it jumped through the air I commented on it to Ron Jon. I asked, "Did you see the scar on the side of that fish?"

He said, "What are you talking about, the scar on the side of the fish? I saw the kingfish jump but I didn't see any scar."

Sure enough we got this kingfish up to the side of the boat and it had this big mark on its side. It was almost like someone had taken an iron and kept it lying on him. It was shocking to Ron Jon that this fish had this mark on its side.

The funny part of that day was Matt Bertuci, "Hey Captain Bouncer, how long you been flying that kite?"

"Thirty of forty years."

A little while later, "You ever catch anything on that kite?"

Matt went fishing with me again this year. We had some memorable trips. We had the roughest swordfish trip I ever went out on in my boat where we beat our way offshore on the roughest day you can imagine. Then we had red hot sword fishing on a relatively calm day because we got out to the north current, then all the way home we had to run in the south current again and it was nasty all the way back. But on the swordfish grounds it was relatively decent and the fish were really biting. Matt still fishes with me today and it's always a pleasure to see him.

Ken Kay Islamorada

Long ago and far far away down in Islamorada there was a boat called *Ken Kay*. The owner was Ken Doubles and believe it or not, his wife's name was Kay. I'll bet that surprised you. But Ken Doubles was a charming old gentleman and we had fished with him on several occasions. So this vacation in June I had my wife Ruth, my brother Flip, my brother-in-law, Mike, and my little sister, Sharon, with me. We were down for a day of offshore fishing targeting mahi mahi and the ever possible shot at a marlin of one kind or another. I had brought some silver mullet I had netted in Miami and had processed for trolling baits. When I got there in the morning I rigged up these trolling mullets. The mate on the boat said, "Those will never work. They won't even swim right."

I said, "That's ok. I'll try them anyway." I was a charter boat captain in Miami and we trolled mullet all the time. We headed offshore and I put my mullet out on a flat line on twenty-pound test. We explained to the mate that we were all very capable anglers and that we wanted to hook our own fish.

It started off very slow in the morning. We picked up a couple of big skip jack tunas. I was fighting one of them, and as it came to the boat it was chopped in half. As I pulled the head half to the boat, here came this giant wahoo, eighty to a

229

hundred pounds, following it back to the boat. So I flipped the skipjack tuna head in the boat and grabbed my twenty-pound outfit with the swimming mullet. The boat was stopped and I started jigging my bait back in. As I jigged my mullet, the wahoo raced across and grabbed my bait and took off around the other side of the boat. Well, my little sister, Sharon, had always talked about wanting to catch a wahoo, so it was my charter boat instinct to jam the rod in her hands and say, "Here' your wahoo."

Unfortunately, as I said that the wahoo raced around the boat and cut the twenty-pound test on the bottom of the boat. It was over before it even started. But it was the first great strike of what would turn out to be a fabulous day. So we trolled on offshore. The dolphin were scarce. I think we caught one or two. I was taking seaweed off my mullet on the left flat line when I caught motion out of the corner of my right eye. There was the mate jerking on the rod on the right outrigger on the opposite side of the boat. The captain, Ken, a very quiet man, was hollering at the mate. And then he called the mate up onto the bridge and read him the riot act. We were down in the cockpit wondering what was going on there. The mate came down off the bridge and said, "Gee, I'm terribly sorry. I saw that white marlin come up on the bait and it was just my natural instinct to try to hook it, but I screwed it up. I should have let you guys do your own thing." So that was a white marlin and it got away.

We went back to trolling and it was another hour or more of no action. It was really a slow day, but all of a sudden my flat line mullet was struck. I ran and grabbed the rod, and as I was dropping back, the left long outrigger got struck. My little brother, Flip, grabbed the rod. I set the hook on my twenty-pound rod, and up came a blue marlin. Flip came tight on his fish, a much bigger blue marlin. Unfortunately his marlin came off on the first jump, but I was tight on mine. I fought the fish for quite a while. It made some beautiful jumps. I had it on twenty-pound test and number six wire, so when I got it close to the boat I called all the shots. I said I would back into the cabin to keep the wire straight as my brother-in-law, Mike, who is a very experienced light tackle fisherman, wired the fish, and then the mate would hit the blue marlin with a flying gaff. Everything went according to plan; we got the fish up to the boat and I kept the wire straight by walking into the cabin. My brother-in-law wired the blue marlin beautifully, fingertips only, and the mate struck the fish in the shoulder with the flying gaff. We put this beautiful little eighty pound blue marlin into the boat.

That one was going straight to Pflueger taxidermy to be mounted and hung on my wall for posterity. What a thrill it was. But I noticed that Ken Doubles was angry. I finally said to Ruth, "You get along good with Ken. Go find out what's the matter. Cool him down. He's usually so mellow." So she was up on the bridge with Ken for quite a while. She just stayed up there watching the world go by, and eventually came back down into the cockpit. She explained that there was a Calcutta in the Islamorada Charter Boat Association for the first boat to catch a blue, a white, and a sailfish in the same day. It had accumulated several thousand dollars. First Ken had chewed the mate out for trying to hook the white marlin instead of letting us catch it. He had blown that. And now he was extra mad because we now had the blue marlin. The blue marlin and the white marlin were the hard part of the Grand Slam. Ken was extra mad because we had blown the white and caught the blue, and hurt his chance to win the Calcutta.

Sure enough, we were trolling back toward home, chugging along at eight or nine knots. For Ken Kay that was really moving. We got a strike and Mike grabbed the rod, and hooked the fish, and don't you know, it was his first sailfish ever. He brought it in and we brought it into the boat to have mounted. He had a sailfish, I had a blue marlin, and the mate had blown the white marlin.

Boy, was Ken mad about the mate blowing that white marlin. But what a memorable day. I can still see that giant wahoo following that skipjack tuna back to the boat and then crashing my mullet. I still can see that blue marlin as Mike wired it up to the boat and the mate gaffed it. I can also still see Ken Doubles up there on the bridge ranting and raving about his lost Grand Slam.

Gary Foreman

I was on my Dusky 33 and I had just hired Michael Green to be my mate for the summer. Michael was a college student, a really great young man, and we were having some good times together. We got a charter from an old, old customer named Gary Foreman. Gary chartered me for several days in a row. When he came fishing with us he explained to me that he had unfortunately had a nervous breakdown. His doctor wanted to put him in a hospital for a while to get his depression squared away. He said he didn't want to be in a hospital, but he promised he wouldn't work, and he wouldn't stay around town. He would go fishing everyday, and he would take his meds as required everyday. He would be a good boy if he could spend his days fishing instead of in the hospital. So, the doctor agreed to allow it.

Gary would show up in the morning. He would give Michael a couple of bags, one with food, one with like a briefcase, one with drinks. Michael would put everything up in the bow and we'd head out. We would go anchor up on a wreck, but it didn't produce much. Drifting over it and bottom fishing I had caught one big red grouper. It's the only fish this wreck had ever produced for me.

So we anchored up and put two baits on the bottom and two flat lines out. Gary sat on the back seat, and in short order we got a bite and we caught a real big mutton snapper. Gary wound on it for a couple of seconds and then said, "I don't feel like fighting it, one of you guys fight it." Michael brought this nice mutton snapper up and we put it in the boat. We baited back up and sent the line back down. It was slick glass calm, and Gary said, "Hey Mikey, would you get me my brief case?"

Mike went up and got him the brief case and brought it back. Gary took something out of the brief case and asked Mike to put it back. Mike returned the brief case to the bow but fifteen or twenty seconds later Gary called, "Hey Mikey, where's the brief case? I need my brief case."

Mike went and got the brief case again and brought it back. Gary put whatever he took out back in the brief case and told Mike to put it back again. So Mike returned the brief case to the bow again. Then we caught another fish, a gag grouper, or a barracuda, mutton snapper, sailfish, we caught everything there. And the fishing turned out to be very good. We caught some really big mutton snappers. All day long Gary would call for his brief case, and then ask Mike to put it back. Then he would ask for his other bag and Mike would bring that. Gary would take something out and ask Mike to put the bag back. He kept doing that with the bag and the brief case. He ran Mike crazy doing this, and he didn't wind in any fish.

Mikey or I would wind in the fish and Gary would sit there in a daze for a while. Then he would tell the greatest sea stories; then he would be in the daze for a while. Then he would tell other stories about helping his daughter maintain her Volkswagen. It was really crazy times. We now call that wreck the Foreman Wreck because of all the great times we had there.

He was a unique guy, Gary Foreman and his tall tales of merchant seamanship, chasing women, and changing oil in his daughter's car. We'll never forget Gary who has since passed away, but had some great times with us.

The Porpoise and Ron Taylor in the Inlet With Snook

I had a couple of guys charter me who claimed they wanted to make a pilot for a TV series. I said they would have to pay me for the trip anyway. It was a pilot and they didn't have all the production plans in place yet. But they wanted to do a pilot TV video on snook fishing in Government Cut. We went out about two hours before dark and the snook were biting really well, and we got a lot of good video. An interesting phenomenon with the snook, in the summertime we would bring a snook up to the boat hooked on a live bait, and anywhere from one to many extra snook will come up with it. This was happening repeatedly this day. Every time we brought a snook to the boat here would come a whole school. We got underwater video, and video off the side of the boat. They were thrilled with all the footage they were getting of these nice twenty-five to thirty-five inch snook we were catching and releasing.

It was getting close to dark, at the very end of twilight, and we had moved from fishing in the ship channel inside the rocks to fishing the north side of the rocks away from the ship channel. The snook were still biting really well. We had a snook up to the boat and there was a whole school of snook with it. And all of a sudden out from under the boat came a full-grown adult bottlenose dolphin. And as he came out from under the boat, he grabbed a snook in his jaws and went flying into the air. It was the most unbelievable thing you could imagine, just shocking to all of us.

It was over as fast as it started, but this big beautiful bottlenose dolphin had grabbed a free-swimming snook right next to the boat. Thank goodness he didn't grab the on with the hook because that would have been a wild charge of drag I'm sure. What a wild shocking event. I've never seen that happen again even though I know that porpoise do eat snook. But that one was a shocker.

While we're on the subject of snook, there was another funny event with the schools of snook coming up to the boat. I had a marine scientist by the name of Ron Taylor who wanted to do some snook tagging in Government Cut. Lisa, our local marine scientist who studied snook for the state, asked if Ron could come down and go out with us and tag some snook. Of course we were glad to have Lisa on the boat anytime we could. She was a lot of fun and a very pretty girl, and we said we would be glad to have Ron go out with us.

About five in the afternoon Ron came out with Lisa. We were on an outgoing tide. We went out to the north jetty of Government Cut and pulled up and started fishing. We weren't getting any bites yet so I asked Ron, "You know, a lot of times when we hook these snook and bring one to the surface, a whole school will come up to the boat with it. We've been told that when that happens we have hooked a female and she is releasing all the eggs and that is exciting the males. She's dispersing eggs because she is in danger, and has all the males coming up to fertilize the eggs."

Ron said he had never heard such a thing and he doubted it seriously. But it is just a phenomenon that happens with snook. At any rate, the snook started biting and we started catching them. We pulled up the first snook, and there were ten snook with it. So we landed the snook and Ron gently squeezed the belly and male fertilizing product came out. He said, "This is a male snook." He put the tag in it and revived it and sent it on its way.

It wasn't long before we hooked another snook and a dozen snook came up with it. He gently squeezed the belly of the snook and the male spawning product came out. He said, "Yep, it's a male snook. I guess your theory about the female snook dropping eggs attracting males isn't working very well."

I said, "Yeah, but we are fishing off South Beach. There's a lot of alternative lifestyle going on here." He had the sickest look on his face. He didn't know what to say.

Ron was a good old boy from the north end of the state, and he didn't want to hear about any alternative lifestyle snook. But it did dispel the claim that these snook were following females up to the boat. That afternoon I think we tagged nine or ten snook. Every time the whole school came up to the boat, every snook we caught was a male. We'll have to find another reason why they all gather together so tightly there in the inlet when we catch one. But either way, it makes for some really great fishing.

Taylor Lapnow's Last Year of High School

At the midterm the dean of Taylor Lapnow's high school up in Connecticut announced a program whereby, in the last grading period, honor roll students would be allowed to use that last grading period on an internship of their choice. Their application and acceptance would be submitted to the dean, and when it was approved they would go to their internship and report back with video and written reports of how their program was going. Their final grade for that grading period would be the quality of their progress throughout the internship.

Taylor had fished with me almost every year since he was six years old. He applied to come down and work as a crewmember on my boat for his last grading period, which was part of April and most of May. He was seventeen years old. He and his older brother, Cody, drove his truck down, and then his brother flew home. I had a vacant condominium for him to use.

At the time I was fishing everyday and nearly every evening. Taylor was helping us out everyday on our trips. He would work with us or ride along, but mostly work with us.

Abie Raymond was my mate, so there were the three of us. We would run daily trips and regular nighttime tarpon trips.

We took Pedro Martinez, the Hall of Fame Baseball player out and caught some beautiful blackfin tunas and sailfish. We hung out with Pedro at the dock on a regular basis. We fished the Miami Dolphins Fishing Tournament and had a wide receiver and special teams coach as our anglers. We thought we had the win in the bag, but at the last minute a guy who had run over to the Bahamas knocked us out of first place into second place. Still we made a big showing for ourselves in that tournament.

Taylor and I went to Joe DiMaggio's Children's Hospital to help set up a program now called Fish to Make Difference, where we took young cancer patients out fishing while they were in recovery. We would take the patient and their families and show them a good time on the boat. It was a reminder for them that there was more to life than the aches and pains, and trials and tribulations for a kid with cancer.

At the end of Taylor's internship Cody flew down to help him drive his truck back. So I took the two boys fishing, just Taylor and Cody and me. Abie took the day off. The three of us went out and Taylor showed off his prowess by throwing his cast net and catching hundreds of pilchards. Then we chummed up a big cero mackerel and some bonitos. They caught numerous fish on fly near what was then Bug Light. We didn't have much luck offshore, but we ended the day at Government Cut and they caught untold numbers of big snook both on live bait and on artificial lures. It was a dream fishing trip for two young men who loved inshore fishing and fly casting. It couldn't have been a better day. It was really phenomenal, and we sent him on his way.

As a sidebar, every week Taylor had to send in a report of how many hours he worked on his internship. On his first week he sent in his report to the dean and it showed eighty hours of work on the boat, which is a good way to get in trouble with the child labor laws. Kids in high school are theoretically not supposed to work more than twenty hours a week. That was what his internship called for, but he had done eighty hours fishing with me. We sure could have gotten trouble with that.

It makes me think back to when I was working on a drift boat. My dad called the crew members and told them that if I went on the boat one more time he was going to have them arrested for contributing to the delinquency of a minor. The two correlate so well I though it was worth mentioning.

Taylor and I had some great times on that internship. Taylor, and Cody, and their father have had some phenomenal trips through the years. The Lapnow family loved to vertical jig, and we would have trips where that was all they would do for two or three days catching amberjacks, and almaco jacks, and red snappers, gag groupers, blackfin tunas, and the list goes on and on. We had some great trips to the Bahamas.

In the Lapnow family Jeff was the father, Cody was the older brother and Taylor was the younger brother. Their beautiful mother was Rachael. She almost never went out on the boat, but would come down to visit us when we came in on many occasions. I love that family. Now Cody has a baby on the way and Taylor is working in the marine industry while Jeff continues with his landscaping business up there in Connecticut. We don't get together as much as we used to, but we'll always have the memories.

Sherman and the Drug Dealer Tuna

Boy, in some ways it's a shame how fishing has changed these days. Sharks have become such an issue where just a few years ago they weren't such a big thing. I was running my boat, Bouncer's Dusky 33, and Sherman Huffman was my mate. He was really a great young man, and we have had a lot of fun together. We had a couple of drug salesmen, legal drugs that is, hosting some doctors in Bimini. It turned out to be the two drug dealers, one girlfriend, and one doctor. They said when the booked the trip that it was yellowfin tunas or bust. They didn't care what it cost, they just wanted to make sure that if at all possible they got into the yellowfin tuna, which is a fifty to seventy-five mile run northeast of Bimini.

We got a load of pilchards and ran up to the north of Isaac's Light and anchored up on the edge. There we caught a bunch of yellowtail snappers. Then, when we had more yellowtails than we knew what to do with, we headed off to the northeast to search for the birds and the tuna that would be underneath them. It didn't take us long to find a flock of birds. We got into them and sure enough we started hooking up on these beautiful yellowfin tuna. They were sixty or seventy pounds apiece. Both of the drug salesmen caught fish, and the guest doctor caught one, and the girlfriend caught a blackfin tuna. Then she caught a yellowfin tuna. Then we had another yellowfin that was bit by a shark, but we still had most of the fish. Then Sherman had caught a tuna too.

The cooler was chock full of tunas and yellowtails. We took all of the ice on the boat and put it on top of the fish and put a few drinks in there to keep them cold. We had a nice watermelon we had to pull out of the ice to make room for all of the fish. So now we were fifty or sixty miles northeast of Bimini and it was about four o'clock in the afternoon. The fish box was full, the watermelon was cold, and nobody wanted to catch another fish. Everybody was eating ice-cold watermelon, and Sherman was sitting on the back of the boat, throwing pilchards out of the live well.

Twenty feet behind the boat yellowfin tunas, fifty, sixty, seventy, eighty pounds were coming up behind the boat and just blasting the pilchards. It was definitely a National Geographic moment. You see these great shows on National Geographic and Blue Planet and you ask, "How can they not fish?" Well, we knew why because everybody's arms were sore – except for mine. So I could not resist anymore. I grabbed a rod, put a pilchard on it and immediately caught a fifty or sixty pound tuna and got it up to the boat. I told Sherman to go ahead and let it go.

He turned to the rest of the group and said, "I told you he was going to release this fish." So I let my tuna go and we sat there until the live well was empty. What an epic event this was. These big yellowfin tunas with bright yellow fins and a bluish cast on their backs jumping out of the water, and boiling on top of the water, eating those pilchards while we ate ice-cold watermelon. Boy it was the thrill beyond thrills.

There is a little anti-climatic finish to this story. We went back to Bimini, and it was still relatively early. I said, "Look guys, we should get some charcoal and some stuff to go with it, and we should cook the tuna on the grill here at the hotel at Seacrest, because the restaurants on the island aren't as adept at cooking tuna. They're more used to cooking snapper and grouper."

I was outvoted. They said, "No we want to go to a restaurant." So Sherman took a big bag of tuna stakes up to the Anchorage Restaurant. He told them that we wanted to have them grilled when we got there at eight o'clock at night, and that there would be six of us. He made it very clear that we wanted them grilled.

When he came back to the hotel we washed the boat then we all got our showers and got dressed. We hiked up the hill and along the Queens Highway until we came to the restaurant. We went in and told them we were there to have that tuna we dropped off earlier. We would have some cracked conch for appetizers and drinks all around while we waited to have the fish cooked. And finally here came this big platter of gray meat. Ugh.

What a heartbreaker. The cook had baked or broiled or whatever she had done. These beautiful tuna steaks had been converted to gray slabs of meat. What a disappointment. Hey, we offered to cook them right there in the hotel. We could have had some sushi and some grilled steaks, but they insisted on going out to the restaurant, and unfortunately we got what we paid for there.

But thank goodness we had plenty more tuna that we took back to Miami and we could cook it any way we wanted. We went from the highest of highs to the lowest of lows when it came to tuna that day.

Planer Marlin

In the summer of 1969 and we were in Bimini with Dan Fulmer as the customer on Randy Lacey's forty-eight foot Lemay charter boat, the *Top Luck*. Randy was very meticulous about his boat. He kept the paint job pristine and the boat was in beautiful condition. He owned a house in South Bimini where we stayed when we were over there. Dan Fulmer was president of the Bimini Big Game Club at the time, and he was going to be our angler for a blue marlin tournament. His brother, Ron, was going to be a ride along guest. Ron would fish on the practice day before the tournament, and the lay day in the middle of the tournament, and if need be, the day after the tournament to try to get him a fish.

During the tournament we did catch a couple of blue marlin. On the practice day and the lay day we didn't catch anything. On the day after the tournament it was flat calm and we weren't catching anything. It was two thirty in the afternoon and Dan's brother was asleep up on the bridge. While he was sleeping we were trolling around. We had a twenty-pound spinning outfit in the left short rigger, rigged with a flying fish, and like all the other baits, it too was being ignored.

Gary and I were down in the cockpit and we decided that Ron needed a wakeup call. I got out a planer, which is a diving device with a metal plate on the front. We clipped that on Ron's line. It pulls very hard, so on a twenty-pound spinner it just started peeling out line. We all started hollering and screaming. Ron woke up on the bridge and dove down into the cockpit and grabbed his rod. He watched as line just peeled off the reel. It ran and ran, and finally when Randy stopped going forward with the boat, and line stopped peeling off the spinner. Ron eventually started gaining line again. Randy put the boat in gear and line started creeping off the reel again. Then Randy took the boat out of gear again and Ron started gaining line again.

As it got close Randy called, "Don't let him cut the transom with his bill. I just painted the transom and it's perfect. Don't let that fish hit the transom with his bill." He was playing the part we were all participating in.

Sure enough, Ron got the leader to the boat, and brought in the wind on leader. The planer popped out of the water and slammed into the transom. And there was the planer firmly dug into the transom of the boat. The planer was a little over two inches wide and made of stainless steel sheet metal. It had driven itself right into the transom of the boat firmly hanging there.

Boy did I get in trouble with Randy over that. But we had some great laughs when Ron Fulmer caught the beautiful planer fish off of South Bimini back in 1969.

Bandar and All Our Great Clients

I like to touch on clients a bit to remind myself of what I learned from them. I have a client named Bandar who is a Saudi Arabian prince. When I finally met him under his terms, he had an entourage of fifteen men watching over him, guarding him, doing his bookings, and his planning and everything. But here's a man of that stature who calls me every month to share his adventures about where he has fished, what he has done for the ecology of his country, and asking what have I been catching. He talks about how his health is, and asks me about my health. Every month a man of that stature calls to say hello. What a great gentleman. Probably his greatest gift to me was to fly me first class to Marseille, France, to go to a world conference on marine reserves and protected areas. I came away with such a rebuilding of my own feelings that the marine reserves are the future of the conservation of the fish; and it has been a driving force in my life ever since.

I might add that my interest in marine reserves was inspired by anther great client of mine, Marty Arostegui. Marty, knowing of my interest in reserves, organized Captain Gill Morotory, and me, and himself to educate South Floridians about marine reserves and protected areas. We've done seminars in numerous locations from the Upper Keys up through Broward and Palm Beach Counties about the marine reserves and protected areas. These are places like national parks where fish can grow to their maturity, congregate in high numbers, and reproduce. And when they are given the opportunity to grow to full size and congregate in good numbers, their spawn not only populates the protected area, but for hundreds of miles around it as the eggs drift off in the Gulf Stream. When fish become too territorial they have to expand beyond their protected area and populate the surrounding areas. So, please jump on board with marine reserves.

Then there's Benji, and Daniel, and Gabriel Hiller from Boston. Benji is another one. He calls every month or so, "Hey Bouncer, called to wish you a Happy Birthday." "Hey Bouncer, called to tell you about my new grandson." "Hey Bouncer. I called to tell you about my tuna trip." "Hey, Bouncer, calling to see when you think we ought to come down for some fishing this year." Benji calls me all the time and I can't tell you how valuable it is.

From all over the world we get texts from all our great customers. I can't name all of you; there are just too many to name all. But I want to thank all of the people from London and Germany, and Canada, and the Pacific Northwest, and the northeast, and the mid west, and north Florida, who share their texts, and emails, and Instagrams and phone calls, and all their contacts. I just love all of my clients and can't thank them enough for keeping us in their lives. You're a great group of people. We love you and thank you so much for everything you do for us in our lives. You really make our lives more fulfilled.

Drug Smuggling in Palm Beach

Back in about 1966, BJ and I had heard about this great run of bonitos that takes place by the Lake Worth Pier in the summer, so we decided we would go up there and get in on the action. I had a white, unmarked, no-window Ford van. On the inside I laid down carpet and put in a bed. Under the bed were rod racks and a couple of big tackle boxes. The van was set up for hauling my gear and being able to rest for a while, and sometimes spend the night. It was really comfortable.

We headed up to Lake Worth Pier probably about four in the morning. We got up there but had no idea where the pier was. We got as close to the beach as we could and started driving on A1A among these great big mansions. We were driving really slow as we looked for beach access. We figured if we could get out to the beach we could look north and south and see the pier. We were going really slow, just creeping along. We got to the end of the road and had to turn around, heading south and continuing to look for the pier.

We came to this red light intersection when police cars came out of the woodwork. Everywhere. I mean there were probably seven or eight police cars surrounding us. I put the van in park and turned it off. They told us to get out of the van; so we got out. One guy took BJ over and started interrogating him. Another guy took me over and interrogated me. Then he had me open all the doors in the van, which I did.

Then he saw this red disk about three eighths of an inch in diameter and an eighth of an inch thick lying on the carpet. He said, "Pick that up and come with me." So I picked up the red disk. He had me carry it in the palm of my hand as we walked over to the officer in charge of the whole scene.

He said, "We've got something going on here. I think it might be drugs."

The officer in charge asked, "What have you got there, son?" He held out his hand and I turned my hand over and dropped the red disk into his hand. Surprise, it had an "M" on the middle of it. He burst out laughing and everybody realized what was going on, and they burst out laughing too, and they sent us on our way.

We found the pier because they gave us complete directions to where we were going. But we caught nothing that morning. It was a total bust for fishing but we got busted for being drug smugglers or something. It made for an interesting story. That's the story of drug smuggling in Palm Beach in my van.